Making Australia Slightly Better Than Average
Again™: Rebuilding Our Common Wealth

Making Australia Slightly Better Than Average Again™: Rebuilding Our Common Wealth

Mark Swivel

PUNCHER & WATTMANN

First published in 2018
Second edition published in 2019

Published by Puncher and Wattmann
PO Box 279
Waratah NSW 2298
http://www.puncherandwattmann.com
puncherandwattmann@bigpond.com

ISBN: 978-1-92578-051-2

Cover photo: Jonathan Miller
Cover design: Adrian Nelson
Typesetting: Christine Bruderlin
Printed by Lightning Source

Australian Government

Australia Council
for the Arts

This project has been assisted by the
Australian Government through the Australia
Council, its arts funding and advisory body.

Contents

---

* A gentle, silly pun that tries to insinuate optimism into this part of the book.

Note you sometimes see at the front of a book

This book is a series of free-range opinions peppered with jokes. It aims to liberate us from the laughable straitjacket of the political status quo. Seriously.

Ed.

For more information visit: thetogetherparty.org.au.

Foreword to Second Edition

What do you do when you think your country has gone mad? I watched with dismay on May 18, 2019 as the reality of a surprising conservative victory set in. Of course Labor ran a poor campaign, confusing and uninspiring, full of verbiage and 'new taxes', led by Bill Shorten, a man too few could believe in. And yes, Scott Morrison ran like a lead singer leaving his band behind for a solo career and executed a neat ju-jitsu, turning the heat on his unseductive opponent. Yes, the ALP thought all it had to do was wait its turn and their reward would be power (the losers!). Yes, the conservatism of Australia is always underestimated. Yes, the widespread anxiety about our material lives is real. Yes, we Aussies have always had ourselves on that we're an egalitarian mob. Yes, religion has never gone away only held its tongue(s?). Yes, a dodgy mining magnate can lawfully skew an election with saturation advertising. Yes, the mainstream media is hopelessly in hock to the powerful, like who knew?! Yes, our voices for change do not reach into the home theatres of Australia. Yes, Bob Brown is a legend who annoys some people. Yes, we are fragmented into tribal echo chambers, our prejudices confirmed daily post by post and like by like, as if we haven't always surrounded ourselves with like-minded people. But, even so, Australia, my country, my beautiful, wonderful country, full of fabulous people and riches, like what the hell?!? How bloody-minded, how utterly determined are we to demonstrate that affluence, peace, space, freedom and education do not guarantee a commitment to a fair society, human rights and the public good? Yes, May 18 saw a bad government returned and a poor opposition dismissed, in a vote that keeps Australia a whole lot less than slightly better than average.

I had expected a narrow Labor win that we'd barely celebrate not a tight Coalition victory that felt like a landslide. Australia faces crises that require urgent action, but nothing in our politics that reflects the emergencies in climate, housing, employment, water and agriculture, governance and corruption. The main takeaway from May 18 is 'business as usual'. Feel the power, people — you've given us a mandate. We were not punished for our incompetence and corruption, we're the government and you're not. Look at the scoreboard. 'Sucked in!'.

Was this really the Climate Election that The Young would win for The Planet? No. Our youth were supposed vote for The Future and wrest power from the ugly machine politicians. But it's social media wish fulfilment that younger voters are defined by climate activism, #me-too and millennial authenticity. Why? Our voters aged 18 to 30 have grown up in 'neo-liberalism'. They have been taught the anxiety of the gig economy, of un-unionised Uber workplaces and non-careers (great for the talented but for others?). They lack any real sense of the collective, mainly because they've been denied its experience, structures and institutions. Think about it.

The May 18 election was the corollary of our contemporary politics — professional and distant — and our re-engineered society — powered by self-interest and competition. It felt like a gigantic act of self-harm — a country voting to stay on the booze and the ciggies to manage its unease because it's the only way to stay sane in a country gone bonkers.

In its bones, Australia is perverse. We do not look at our beauty — our landscape, rivers and forests, our people and animals — and say, we must honour this glory above everything else, yes! Instead, when we vote, enough Australians says we must maintain our material comforts above all, to protect us from the uncertainty lurking in our hearts, and we can risk damaging this beauty and bounty — and each other — while we are at it. Because in our hearts we don't quite know what all this beauty around is for or what we really believe. But please don't tell anyone, because it's a terrifying prospect — as scary as a country in permanent drought. Go to work, look after your family and hope it all works out!

Then there is God. The unbelievable ascension of belief! Yet religion is back on centre-stage precisely because our way of life does not feed our souls well enough. We watch fantasy tv about singing and 'finding our voice' because we are not finding it elsewhere. We obsess about property and home renovation because what's inside our homes is not clear. Australians take heroic quantities of anti-depressants, get pissed and do drugs in ways that tell us all is not well. We have never settled here in this land. And the result for many is God. Or more TV. Or booze. Australia's real crisis lies outside politics. Policy 'issues' betray deeper challenges. I've long thought the real reason 'white' Australia doesn't connect with our indigenous people is shame — a sense that we don't know who we are, why we are here and what we are doing with this land. Less racism than a lack of spiritual confidence and knowledge.

So now we have a politics that is all about Aspiration, Tax Cuts, and Religious Freedom. By the way, no one lacks the freedom to worship — there is no persecution here but we did seem to once agree that religious belief is subject to democratic norms. Of course government should ensure that ordinary people live prosperous lives, but a politics limited to that is the definition of poverty! But Aspiration — what does it even mean? Little more than the right to accumulate wealth as an absolute goal for yourself and your family, to place the personal above the social, the private over the collective. It is the privatisation of politics. The death of politics. Labor pulls the wrong rein following the Coalition to the right. The Australian Labor Party committed to Aspiration the day it removed the U from the party's name. Hawke and Keating continued it in their assault on unionism in the Accord in 1983. Labor has supported Aspiration every day it has failed to take on the class warfare waged by Australian conservatives over the last generation.

So now Albo, Anthony Albanese, leads the ALP — a man who once staged sit-ins at Sydney University to defend the study of political economy — Marx and Miliband, Galbraith and Sen — because he knew economics was less about supply and demand than the realities of Power. Albo knows the ordinary lives of Australians and where he comes from but in his opening exchanges he has looked the wrong way. Albo needs to reconnect with his younger self. The son of a single mum. The supporter of a football team, South Sydney, that's all about 'community'. The fan of edgy music — punk or new wave — that was about shaking up the world. Albo should not be singing the song of Aspiration, because that way lies oblivion for any party wanting to bring people together and create a better, fairer country. We should aspire to be better, more ambitious than Aspiration. Part of that is developing a bolder vision for Australia based on more than mining, banking and shopping; a vision of Australia powered by renewable energy, technology businesses and new agriculture.

Let's be clear. Sco-Mo fought hard and well. He took massive risks — even with the forces supporting him. It should be a lesson to the ALP that real risks carry real benefits. But our freshly elected PM is a fraud — look no further than rugby league for evidence! Boofy blokes follow their teams for life in the suburban tribalism of footy. I've followed Easts since Russell Fairfax debuted in 1974 after defecting from Randwick Rugby Club. Morrison claims to be a Sharks fan but grew up in Bronte and should've stayed with Easts, now the Sydney Roosters. No one calls him on it. Why? Probably because it's all nonsense — like so much of our affected Aussieness. Our commitment to these things is skin-deep. And on the paradoxes go like Russian dolls. We have no story, no real shared spirit, so we are prey to fear and a leader who prays.

Inevitably, Tax Cuts were the first act of our new parliament. Looked at in micro, tax cuts make sense, to boost consumer demand after wages have flatlined for so long. After all government controls little else now.

Sure it remains a huge employer and investor — with our federal budget equal to a third of GDP. With interest rates set by the Reserve Bank and wages handled by the Productivity Commission, tax cuts are the main 'residual' policy tool in the hollowed out neo-liberal state. But enhanced demand is not the only result. Tax cuts undermine the creation and funding of public services and assets. Then it gets worse.

The tax cuts just passed unwind progressive taxation, the idea that the better off among us should chip in more for the greater good. It powered the flourishing of democracies from the USA to Sweden in the second half of the twentieth century including our own. The flattening of tax scales defines the greater good as cash in the hand rather than a constructive state creating a better society. And this happens with no debate on how to get capital — especially big companies — to pay their way. We should be unwinding the privileges of corporate tax minimisation and the light touch royalties we get from minerals exploration. Instead we pay off the average citizen with buttons and the homeless and jobless, our dry rivers, the poorly educated, our swelling jails and misfiring markets can wait. All these things will worsen without enlightened government, properly funded. Sit back and watch. Fiscal Phobia is the great, tragic achievement of modern conservatism — because taxation is the foundation of redistributive justice.

We have enabled a government with a slim majority to undo what it took generations to achieve. Congratulations, Australia! And Labor voted to support this train wreck. Yet it's not just Labor's fault, but all our faults. It's the fault of everyone who turned away from Politics as the story we all tell to history. Every time Politics has been written off as too dull or divisive to discuss at a dinner party or barbie, we have died a little. The children of Whitlam — my mob — have snuggled into the wealth and power structures of our society and allowed this to happen — because the fate of others, of the majority of Australians, matters far too little to us to do much about. We flatter ourselves with micro-projects we say are about 'giving back'. If we want feedback on our choices, look to May 18. The ultimate prize of our adult decisions is tax cuts and the dismantling of our democracy.

So, what next? What is the 'answer'? A deeper Story that speaks to the fears of ordinary people. That is what the conservatives did in this election, in a shallow way. Progressives need to find their own story, tell it to everyone, including those who did not vote for them this time round and probably won't next time. GetUp wasted millions in 2019 on negative personal campaigns when a more constructive narrative was required. The professional apparatchiks of Labor somehow missed what was happening — not just in Queensland but across New South Wales and beyond. The Story should tell how we live in interconnected communities, that no one does anything alone, that we are all much more the same than we are different, that many of us suffer more than we realise, that we allow the strong and wealthy to lord it over us (and that's unAustralian!). The Story should restore political economy and the constructive fiscal state to the heart of government because inequality is real and needs action. The Story needs a longer term vision of economic development — how will Australia live and prosper on this dry continent, powered by renewables, technology, agriculture and trade with the world. Developing the Story will take patience and kindness and time. A process of education, of listening, of sitting with each other. So I will now take a long walk on the beach and have a think about how to begin. I look forward to talking with you somewhere soon because we can only return to the task of Making Australia Slightly Better Than Average Again™ — together.

Mark Swivel
7 July 2019

PART ONE:
Hello, people of Australia

Let me explain . . .

My name is Mark Andrew Swivel. I guess with a surname like ours Mum and Dad thought we'd better give him a couple of truly boring first names. They succeeded.

I am a Near Dead White Male. 52. Lawyer for a living (low-flying). Humourist for fun (quite amusing). Cricketer (average). Chorister (Russian). Ocean swimmer (semi-retired). Husband. Father. Brother. And so on. I love music, sport and books and think Australia needs to change.

Look, I'm as busy as you are, but I've turned off the telly and put my phone in the fridge so I can write this book . . . because we need to fix this country and our politics.

In short, we need **#auspol*** to be much more like the Australian people, like you and me.

---

* Interwebs shorthand for Australian politics

I reckon that the time has come for us to rise up and Make Australia Slightly Better Than Average Again™.

To put it another way, we have left our Common Wealth on the barbie and it's nearly burnt to a crisp. But we can save it if we act now.

Are you with me on this, People of Australia?

Write your answer here. Neatly.

If the answer is YES, please continue in an orderly fashion to the next page.

If the answer is NO, thank you for buying the book and enjoy your life.

PART TWO:

Forward! The direction in which we must head

Australia is as blessed as it is broken. We are as wretched as we are beautiful. We have lost our way and our leaders offer no real story of The Future. Australia is now run by The Wealthier People at the Expense of The Not So Wealthy. We have lost sight of our Common Wealth. The things we share and enjoy together. In my book, that is not on. In fact it's dead set Un-Australian. #Auspol's perpetual antagonism over trivia obscures the need for real change.

The question for us, the People of Australia, is what are we going to do about this pickle we're in? I'm going to run for the Senate. With your support, I would like to join that shower of truly unrepresentative swill to make it look and act a little more like us. I have the crossbench in my crosshairs. This book tells you how and why I have decided to do this mad, unlikely thing (the odds of success are up there with finding life on Pluto but I am determined). I am looking for like-minded people across Australia to get involved somehow, to join me and help fix this place . . . whatever it takes.

Along the way I'll rant quite a lot about what's gone wrong with Australia and how we might turn it around. I don't know that much but I do know lots more than many in elected office. And that is as sad as it is funny. But you learn a thing or two from working as a grass-roots lawyer, from running football clubs and circuses, from doing comedy shows, singing in choirs and barely making the finishing line in ocean swimming races. The main thing you learn is that the political class detached from the rest of us a long time ago and has no real idea of what it is doing beyond preserving itself. The urgency of this moment in our history is clear. The problem is not Left or Right or one person or another. It's the whole damn show! And it will not fix itself.

We talk a lot about populism today. I truly believe we have the wrong kind of populism. We have nut jobs ready to drum up fear and loathing about immigration and refugees or gender politics and so-called Australian values. Yet I think We The People want a country that is fair and has a clear idea of its future. Australia is far more inclusive and welcoming than the media often portrays. Most of us are decent and dull, in a good way! The best way. My kind of populism is about making communities worth living in, of building a future where government serves us and not the market, where the test is always 'so, tell me how does this bring people together?' An Australia that is Slightly Better Than Average . . . like the one I grew up in, when kerb and guttering was new and exciting, when we had free university education, a sane housing policy, and we all seemed to be part of a national adventure.

Before we go any further, have a little think about what YOU might do to help Make Australia Slightly Better than Average Again™ . . . go on . . . I am a reasonable person. Just like you. I know you've been busting a gut at work. And you need to help your kid with quadratic equations . . . or pretend to. They're tough, aren't they? There's dinner to cook or take-away to pick up. A great new crime series you need to catch up on. Then there's the Tigers game. It's going to be a cracker. I'll be watching myself.

But after all that. You have a little time. An hour or two. To chip in. You know it! To do something to help Make Australia Slightly Better Than Average Again™. You can start by reading this book and voting for me at the next election. But then what?!? An angry social media post or signing an online petition won't cut it. They're not listening in Canberra.

Here's a box for you to write your Preliminary List of Things I Can to Do to Make Australia Slightly Better Than Average Again™.

Go on . . . cut loose!

Why the humour?

Because things are so serious. Because the river bed of our nation is dry. And humour can bring the rain. It's a nice line, isn't it? And I believe it.

I'd like you to read the book. That's why it's written like this. Humour is fundamental to how we talk to each other in ordinary life and our politics should reflect that. Of course it's fun to laugh at the powerful and the absurdities of political life. It's a basic human need. But what if we had a laugh at the outrages around us and then did something?

We need new ways of thinking and doing politics. Humour can be part of that. It might even help people get interested in politics again (am I dreaming?!?). People don't join political parties anymore. The majors claim to have around 50,000 members each. By contrast, Richmond Football Club has 100,000 members! More than twice as many. But what's stopping us from getting involved in the democracy of our own country? Honestly? Nothing and no one. Why do we put up with this nonsense? If we want to Make Australia Slightly Better Than Average Again™ the ball — that dog-eaten tennis ball of destiny — is clearly in our court. Join a party, start a party, protest in the streets, run for parliament, do a sausage sizzle for your favourite candidate. Just get into it!

Why do we need to do something?

Because a coup is in progress. It's been happening for a long time, quietly, invisibly. I'm not a mad conspiracy theorist. I'm a boring community lawyer who loves sport. I still play cricket (third grade) and football (sevenths). Not that well, but at least I turn up! But what do I mean by a coup? There are no generals in this type of coup. It's a different operation. A war is being waged on government in itself. Not by this particular government. Not by any particular party. But by the whole political class through the apparently endless process of privatisation, outsourcing and deregulation. It's been going since the 1980s. And even worse the process is speeding up to the point that we have lost faith in government and that is a very dangerous thing indeed, because government is the main way we 'do' democracy.

So, what is Government? It's the way we pool resources to do things for people, for us. All of us. From fixing potholes to national health policy, from keeping the local swimming pool clean to funding scientific research. It is how we build our Common Wealth. Government is not just the military and border control and subsidies for business, or tax breaks for people who don't really need them. Government can do — and does — a huge range of things for all of us. But you never really hear it talked about like that do you? Australia — in fact the whole of the so-called Western world — is on a massive downer about Government. Government is a bit like the team-mate no one passes the ball. We're passing the ball to The Market instead. And who is benefitting from that Lifestyle Choice? Huh?!?

To me Government is how we build communities. Government is an essential part of You and Me, of our way of being Us. But we have let that idea of Government slip. We starve it of money because we are told we need tax cuts more than anything else. And, to remind you of an awkward truth, most countries in most elections over the last generation or two have voted for tax cuts without realising they have been unwinding Government — and their democracies — in the process. But that's the truth of it. We were sold only the upside of privatisation and tax cuts. Now we are paying the price — literally in higher prices but more dangerously in the loss of influence over economic and social development. Privatisation is not always bad, by the way, but it should not be the basis of a civilisation. As you begin this book, it's important to remember that Government is us.

Why do we need to act NOW?

There was a moment in mid 2018 when #auspol became 'too silly for words' as my mum said when she saw my first sad attempt at a New Romantics haircut in 1982. First, a Senator from Queensland, Pauline Hanson, tried to sack one of her party members for sticking to a tax policy she'd been spruiking herself only a few days earlier. Then, Barnaby Joyce, former husband and Deputy PM, appeared on prime time TV with his new partner and bub to complain about all the damn media attention they were getting. And got paid for it. Excuse me?! Soon after, another Senator, David Leyonhelm, told a colleague to 'stop shagging blokes'. Whereupon Mark Latham, one-time ALP leader, threatened to return to politics to save Australia from 'political correctness, identity politics and anti-white racism'. Because they are the real problems facing us today, right?

While I've been writing this book Senator Fraser Anning has called for a return of the White Australia Policy and a ban on Muslim immigration. Essentially to get everyone's attention. It worked. All year, a leading government minister, Peter Dutton, has talked endlessly about African gangs, immigration and stopping boats while our urbane, educated, now ex-prime minister Malcolm Turnbull did nothing to stop him. Meanwhile the opposition was too busy playing small-target politics to inspire anyone, happy to watch the Coalition government implode as it scored own goal after own goal. None of this shameful carry-on addressed the serious issues facing Australia like our long term prosperity, the national housing crisis, how we educate ourselves, renewable energy and climate change, youth unemployment, the withering of the rule of law, or justice for indigenous communities, to name a few things our political class might be focussing on in their spare time.

And then at the end of a long winter, the elected Australian government decided to eat itself alive in a display of self-harm and self-indulgence not even a mother could forgive. Replacing yet another PM meant the government was repeating the mistakes of its opponents and left a nation traumatised without so much as a toll-free counselling line to help us process this pointless nonsense. As we go to print the government has not even explained why it was necessary to change its leader. It just, um, well, did it. Like a child explaining why it flour-bombed a lollipop lady on the last day of primary school. Um, well. Err . . . Dutton wanted to be PM. The hardliners didn't like Turnbull or renewables. The long-suffering deputy of the Libs, Julie Bishop, was ignored and we ended up with a default candidate.

When the dust settled, Australia had Scott Morrison as its prime minister. The would-be man of the people who, when immigration minister, told us that our government 'does not discuss on-water operational matters', who, as treasurer, resisted a royal commission into our banks for years then pretended he was tough on them, and who recently swore blind that we'd go broke without huge corporate tax cuts, then when the Senate knocked him back pretended it didn't really matter. Morrison now wanders the nation leading an incoherent and divided government hoping the voters will buy his football-loving, church-going, suburban bloke routine. He strikes me as an unctuous vacuum-cleaner salesman. A poor man's Bob Hawke with no vision or new policies, making a bad thing worse. Yet the problem is not Morrison, rather the culture that has produced him.

So Australia needs help. Heaps of it. From We the People. Our politics has stopped making sense. Our parliamentarians are a joke, with honourable exceptions. After a year touring a political satire show around comedy festivals, pubs and clubs, I came to the considered view that we need better people: people with a sense of humour . . . people like us in parliament to replace the jokers we currently have.

Even me. God help us! And I reckon the crossbench is the place to be. A place where you can join the national conversation and make a bit of a difference. I encourage everyone, all of you, especially younger people, to get involved, to do something yourselves. The party system should not be the gatekeeper of our democracy. Australia is full of top people and it's a bit odd so few of them make it into parliament.

The Book in Brief

Here's my main point, just in case you don't want to read the rest of the book. Australia has a serious problem beneath the pantomime of our politics. Almost every policy, every major decision made by governments of all shapes and flavours, during my adult life — from the mid-80s to now — has favoured The Market over Government. Education, health, electricity, aviation, banking, child care and employment services have all been privatised or outsourced wherever possible. It is the reflex of conventional policy across the western world. The actual purpose of Government now is to give way to The Market. There is a grim consensus on this among the major parties of the major democracies. And every step of the way the People of Australia have been told it is all for the best. But it's not.

For starters, this approach to government shows a remarkable lack of self-esteem from the very people we elected for the very purpose of *doing* government. This country shouldn't be run by The Market. Because The Market doesn't look after us, it looks after itself. Because that is what The Market is designed to do. The Market of course is just a bunch of guys in suits hoping not to get found out. Our politicians have taken their hands off the wheel and said, 'go for it, let The Market decide, sounds great, takes the pressure off us!' The result is that Australia is now run by and for The Wealthier People at the expense of The Not So Wealthy. Consider the housing crisis. Youth and regional unemployment. Consider wages growth or the lack of it. Think about electricity prices or university fees. Look around, People of Australia, and ask yourself: can you rely on The Market to look after you? Write your answer in the margin, there's plenty of space for the word 'NO'.

Like anything, Government can be rubbish, slow and hopeless. But Government can be good. Government is not inherently inefficient. Government is not all bad. Government doing things — owning things and managing them — does not mean Australia becomes Soviet Russia as some suggest. Government, for all its faults, built this country and we need to bring it back. We need to invest in Government. Not for everything but for loads more than it's doing now, and for the things We The People want it to do.

I believe we can redirect our politics towards building our Common Wealth. And what's that? The stuff that exists and works for all of us. From our roads to our regulators. From renewable energy to reconciliation. Our measuring stick for our politics and government policy and action should then be: how does it deliver the greatest good for the greatest number? We can rebuild our idea of Government, of politics, of the way we run this country . . . and for whom. Above all, We The People need to start talking about this and seeing ourselves — personally and collectively — as part of the solution. Impotent whinging doesn't suit us Australians. It's time for us to get involved. That is the starting point of the long road to Making Australia Slightly Better Than Average Again™.

You might like to make a note or doodle here now to express the slightly trickier than average thoughts and feelings you may be experiencing.

Our Common Wealth

That's right. Not mine. Not yours. Not MyKi. Not My Health Care.
Not My School. Our Common Wealth. What's that? Most of the stuff
outside your house. Your local pool, our beaches, the roads and our
schools. Our public life and the things that make it. Our courts and the
public service. Our national parks and the minerals underneath. Our
libraries and sports fields. Our laboratories and council depots. Our
hospitals and fly-blown showgrounds. Our nature strips and airports.
All the things that make our lives and communities, our businesses and
our families, function and worthwhile. That is our Common Wealth.
Some of it might be privately owned but even then public funding is
always important, or has been, in making it happen. You may already
be thinking that we don't talk about the world around us like this very
much these days. We might notice when things are not there, but do we
talk about how we might pass the hat around to make things better? Not
much. Not really. But we should. We should have another look at Our
Common Wealth, how it got there and how it stays there.

Here's the thing. We humans — even Aussies — are social creatures,
aren't we? Sure, you've never met the curious family that lives at
number 17. I know you have a co-worker who sits in silence through
team meetings chewing mints you've never seen at the newsagents.
Bit of an odd-bod. But we are not seven billion individuals living in
splendid isolation from each other, are we? We are not even 25 million
individuals living separate lives in a country called Australia. We are
so much more than that. We are all defined by the people we love and
work with. If others ceased to exist so would we. They make us who
we are. Ignoring the odd genuine sociopath, most of us are completely
intertwined with the needs, desires and sometimes quite irritating
personal habits of other people. Yes, we have been encouraged to see
ourselves — and human nature itself — as being essentially competitive
and individualistic. But that's garbage. Competition and individualism

do not define us as people and communities. We are other people. At the end of the day. And at the beginning.

Our politics should reflect the basic truth of our inter-connectedness and inter-dependence. But it doesn't. Politics, like life, needs to be about other people and how we treat them. Instead it's all about The Economy with Competition as the primary virtue. Who really wants their life to be a rolling episode of *Australia's Got Talent* or *Master Chef*, producing one winner a year from thousands of excited but ultimately disappointed contestants? Our lives should be more like the scene in that old Harrison Ford movie *Witness* where the Amish folk raise a barn together. Aw, shucks. Yet we are in thrall to the Great God, The Economy, which has us all competing, out for ourselves, pursuing our own material goals. We are expected to make offerings and sacrifices, to walk on eggshells so we don't annoy our God. But we need The Economy to serve us, not the other way round. Our politics should be about how we build communities to work for us. It should be about how we live together on and with this planet.

By the way, Our Common Wealth is not socialism, communism or a third way. For starters, abolishing private property is wild wishful thinking, like opening the bowling for Australia was for me as a kid. Those ideas belong to a previous time (for starters, I can only bowl very ordinary off-spin these days). Karl Marx wrote *Das Kapital*, his analysis of capitalism, 170 years ago! It's not exactly an instruction manual on what to do, but more a rambling rant on how The Not So Wealthy are oppressed and ripped off. Do we need Marx to work that out? Doubt it. The thing is, the way we live today is something new. The working class is different. Workers are united more by consumption than working in factories. Few call themselves working class anymore. We are treated as Consumers not Citizens. As Spectators rather than Actors. You might call our current social order: Spectacle Consumerism, but that sounds a bit fancy.

Private property will always be part of our society but we need to get back to thinking about how we develop public property, public services and institutions. We need to rebalance our society. We need to take the car to the tyre guy for a wheel alignment. The way I see it the tide has run one way over the last 30 years toward The Market, and it needs to run back the other way towards We The People. My preferred name for this way of thinking and doing politics is Our Common Wealth. What's yours?

Write it down in the box below . . .

Unpicking The Status Quo

People of Australia, I should warn you that I'm not especially interested in the individuals who currently run our political system. We are far too concerned with personalities. I am mainly interested in the whole show — in the ball not the wo/man, the issues not the identities — because I was taught to think that way at the good state school, Sydney Boys High, that I went to from 1978 to 1983. Incidentally, the current PM also went there. Sco-Mo's parents did the wardrobe and make-up for our school musicals. But I digress.

I am, optimistically, interested in encouraging new ways of thinking about where we're at. Most of my ideas will probably be familiar from the conversations you have with actual people in real life. At the pub or bus stop. Here's what I think about where we are at right now.

- Our current government is a gaggle of chancers who favour The Wealthier People over The Not So Wealthy, hate unions with the mania of angry children who won't eat their vegetables, believe in The Market above everything else (except when it suits them not to) and seem to believe in a punishing kind of Christianity that sees The Poor as losers. These people regard not having money or a job as a character defect rather than the inevitable outcome of a system that puts profit before humans and deliberately concentrates wealth in a minority of the population. And the zealous young insects coming through their ranks know nothing about history or human suffering and are a serious worry! Our modern society did not spring from a textbook written by Hayek, you know. It was formed by blood, sweat and tears, mainly that of workers.
- Meanwhile, the current Opposition accommodates conservative views and policies because they're frightened that genuinely alternative policies won't win them an election. They placate The

Wealthier People to try to secure power and campaign funding and advance their personal careers. They are way too timid, allowing conservatives to define the ludicrously narrow terms of what passes for debate. They are effectively telling The Not So Wealthy who usually vote for them: 'Suck it up, folks, this is the best we can do in an ugly world'. They're also terrified of being confused with the Greens (who struggle to get 10 per cent of the vote even though the planet's on fire). On most major issues like energy, tax and border control the opposition has been far too close to the government — only an inch away — for far too long.

What Does the Future Look Like?

This is the unarticulated question in the hearts and minds of many voters. Why is the weather on the news? Will it rain on the weekend? Is my job going to be swept away when a tropical cyclone hits The Economy? Why is the price of tapis crude reported on the news every day? Actually, I have no idea! But if you find out, let me know (I'm asking for a mate who drives a bit for Uber and dabbles in day-trading).

Politics is really about The Future — what it might look like, how it might hurt us, how we can prepare for it. Put another way, politics is the art of managing or manipulating the fear of disaster that lurks in our hearts. Of losing a job, a business, a marriage. At its best politics allows the odd dream, however deluded it may turn out to be, but it is mainly about fear.

I reckon we currently have no politics of The Future. Our politics takes place in a weird, suspended, empty present. Debates and scandals come and go in a chaotic blur. Before you get your head around one story, another appears to bemuse and confuse, to outrage or perplex. The only constant is leadership speculation. There is no real plan, no memory, no accountability. Without a vision of The Future, politics is pointless. It's one of the reasons so many of us have tuned out.

Ask yourself what story are the political class telling us of The Future? The best answer is this: more of the same, folks, with minor tweaks — free kicks for business if you vote one way, a little more cash for schools and hospitals if you vote the other. There is no real story of The Future, nothing to manage the underlying, understandable, mortal fear that lurks in our hearts.

In my humble, evidence-based opinion, none of this is good enough for We The People. And it is our fault because we have voted these scallywags in, time and again, and we do nothing serious to try to change it. Occasionally we might vote for an Independent (and we could do more of that), but this predicament is pretty much our fault and ours to fix. Let's get on with it.

Proposing not Opposing

Some readers might mistake me for a Progressive — even a leftie ratbag — because I support the reorganisation of society in the service of The Not So Wealthy rather than The Wealthier People. Yet Progressives tend to focus on opposing things, and right now we need to be proposing. We need to think about governing and what we as a country would do if given the reins of power. It's good to protest, don't get me wrong. Protesting is good and necessary. History tells us that if there had been no opposing over the years, we'd have no democracy. Full stop. However, Rebuilding Our Common Wealth depends on working out how to govern. Proposing. For all of us.

Progressives can also make the mistake of thinking their arguments speak for themselves. They sometimes dismiss fellow citizens who think differently from them as bad guys who should be ashamed of themselves, rather than arguing the issues at hand. Worse, progressives can retreat from the political fray, enjoying protesting and arguing among themselves over the 23 million options for change. Sound familiar? I've done it myself. So, perhaps it's better not to think about being Progressive, or Left or Right. Let's think instead about All of Us and our Common Wealth. 'What does that mean?!?' I hear you cry ... well, read on!

It's time for Disruption

Politics is way too important to be left to politicians. But I do feel a little sorry for them (ok, not much). Our current system with its three-year spin cycle of elections means our so-called representatives operate in disabling anxiety. In constant fear of losing their seats and their jobs. We should not overlook the fact that most parliamentarians — the best and the worst — make sacrifices to get elected. Most give up alternative careers. As a result, many would sell their relatives to stay in parliament so they can feed their families. It's a bit of a paradox. But it's not a system designed to serve We The People, as we all know.

Disruption. You've probably heard that term. It's what the internet did to newspapers. What Uber did to taxi companies. What Netflix did to television. Disruption is everywhere. Except politics. Let's change that. This Whitepaper-Roadmap-Blueprint for Building Our Common Wealth is intended as a Manual for Disruption. My campaign for the Senate is hands-on disruption. We need to get out of the house and get into the House. Howzat?!? And let's have lots of small parties and independents in parliament. We should not have a cartel operated by the major parties. To borrow the language of the Market, we have a rigid oligopoly where we need genuine competition.

And much as I love it, satire does not seem to be having much impact on Australia. Perhaps we need a Royal Commission into political humour and its failure to transform our society. It's almost like it's achieved nothing. Like ever. All those excellent jokes from terrific comedians — Micallef, Crabbe, *The Juice* — and so little to show for them. So it's come to this. We The People need to take control of #auspol.

About this Book

First up you can see my humorous vision to Make Australia Slightly Better Than Average Again™ in the *Executive Summery* in Part Three. It's fully costed. See the section on Fiscal Rectitude to allay your fears about my commitment to economic responsibility. This part of the book is based on the political satire show I've toured over the last year from Melbourne to Alice Springs, from Mullumbimby to Sydney. It is designed to entertain and get you thinking about how we can do politics differently. Hint: it's not an Executive Summary.

If you want the Serious Meat of my looming Senate campaign, head straight to *Part Six: Seriously. Fixing Australia*. It's an outline of policies that I think Australia should pursue to build its Common Wealth. Many will read this section and think 'ah, that's not possible, we could never fund that'. To which I say, costing is important but we need to break the frame of debate. Tax is not bad. Tax is the means of investing in social justice by building public assets and services. Tax cuts largely deliver private profits and much less benefit than we are sold. Tax needs to be done better. Be warned — it's not for the faint-hearted and you might like a few giggles over a Pinot, with a chunk of manchego and the odd seedless grape before you get there. Or you might like to start thinking about how to refine and extend the policies to help me get elected! Either way, if I do make it to the Senate, *Part Six: Seriously. Fixing Australia* shows you how I would vote and campaign for change.

In a nutshell, I want to see the return and restoration of Government in the public interest — from public broadcasting to a national ICAC, from stopping privatisation to long-term industry policy, from boosting legal aid to going long on scientific research. Government as an active, constructive force for positive change. How does that sound?

Now you might like to doodle an abstract figure. Your totem animal. A sensual torso. Whatever helps you manage the nervous cerebral energy we hope this book generates.

Stop Press.

Yep. It really is time for humourists to admit we cannot compete with the real thing. #Auspol is just too funny in its grim, unfunny way. While editing the print copy of this book, the Coalition government decided to support a motion in the Senate that 'it was ok to be white', to move our embassy from Tel Aviv to Jerusalem, and to more or less officially pretend that climate science remains a matter of conjecture. In a few days. The government then lost its blue riband seat of Wentworth to an independent as a punchline. It's better than anything *The Onion* can do. And as good as he is, what's the point of John Birmingham's hilarious invective? Who knows what will have happened by the time you are reading this? It's time to act, to use humour to bring about actual change in #auspol.

PART THREE:
Executive summery*: How to Make Australia Slightly Better Than Average Again™

Warning: this section contains satirical faux policy proposals but, as often happens with satire, some of the content might make you think 'actually, that's not a bad idea'. In fact most of these ideas are pretty close to what I actually think anyway as you'll see later on in Part Six: Seriously. Fixing Australia. This material was originally developed for the comedy show cum rolling focus group called Alternative Prime Minister that I toured in 2017–18.

1. Responsible Service of Capitalism

Capitalism has generated extraordinary wealth and extraordinary suffering. All at once. All over the world. For a good couple of centuries. Many people today drive amazing cars with cup holders and seat warmers. Some of us have enormous houses full of lovely rugs and throw cushions. Our houses almost run themselves. Most Australians can now forget to turn off the lights from their smart phones. If they want to. It's incredible! If only our houses were self-cleaning. It won't

---

* Not a typo but a gentle pun, remember, to insinuate positive energy!

be long. Yes, millions across the globe have been dragged out of the grinding poverty that has persisted for most of human history, even if they have mostly been dragged from their villages into call centres, factories and urban slums.

Yet for all the wealth Capitalism has created, it is currently out of control and needs to pull its head in. In my humble, evidence-based, opinion it is unequal, unfair and unsafe. Toxically so. Even in an Australia that often seems like one big shopping mall full of shiny consumer goods, with its suburbs of beautifully renovated houses endlessly appreciating in value, our wealth is far too unevenly distributed and too many people are being excluded from too many things — jobs, education, home ownership, even nightclubs.

We The People worry about safety all the time. We can all see the warning signs in our parks and streets and venues telling us what we can and can't do. The Nanny State some call it. We worry about drunks in pubs. We turned Sydney's Kings Cross into a joyless wasteland by closing the joints we used to have fun in. We insist on the responsible service of alcohol on safety grounds and we should extend this policy to The Economy, which is far more dangerous than idiot drinkers. Profits are too high and wages are too low. Executive salaries are crazy. We need a new balance. Speed limits for The Economy. Not a strait-jacket but a seat belt. After all, if people are paid a bit more they can buy more stuff. Maybe even a house. Wouldn't that be nice? Or a flat, let's not get carried away. A studio apartment. I'm a realist.

Yes, it's time for the Responsible Service of Capitalism. Time to say to our titans of industry, 'Hey, Rupert, Gina, Frank, you've had enough, time to go home'. It is time for The Miners, The Banks, The Shopping Malls of Australia to share the love — by which I mean money — with the people who work to make those profits. The jaffle-iron demonstrators from Chadstone to Chermside, the pearl divers of Broome, the sheep drenchers of Wilpena Pound and the beard oil wholesalers of Fitzroy. Yes, even tattooed, over-pierced, chia-seeded, turmeric-latte drinkers! Without the workers of this country, The Mines, The Banks and The Shopping Malls make no money at all. None. Lest we forget, this basic truth of business seems to have completely disappeared from human consciousness.

Incidentally, why, friends, does ripping stuff out of the ground pretty much remain our only big idea for making money? Like, what's the plan, fellas? Can the country survive forever on coal mining, home renovations and flogging private health insurance or retail super fund plans that don't work as well as the non-profit alternatives they were meant to replace?

So People of Australia, I call this policy Responsible Service of Capitalism. It looks like this:

- The Not So Wealthy need to be paid properly and not just on Sundays.
- Companies must pay a fair share of tax instead of always sooking they're overtaxed.
- Workers must be able to bargain and strike so they are citizens and not beggars.
- Smaller business is where it's at — our newsagents and video stores will save us!*
- Capitalism needs to work with nature instead of treating it like a cat's scratch pole.
- And one day we might have a bit of a chat about where The Economy is going . . .

---

*This joke highlights the vulnerability and crazy-brave headspace of small business people across our nation. Phone stores, pie shops and nail salons are all mad leaps of faith that we need to embrace and nurture.

Add your own policy ideas or doodles for **Responsible Service of Capitalism** here. Go for it!

2. Fair Dinkum Law Enforcement.

Our politicians spend an awful lot of time talking about law enforcement and terrorism and gangs and bikies and ice fiends. It's almost like they want We The People to be scared. Of course, when laws are broken they need to be enforced. But this should apply to all laws, not only the laws that apply to The Not So Wealthy. We have a massive blind spot: the Top End of Town. The people responsible for The Market and The Economy. The Economy that produces a few winners and too many losers. The Economy that makes housing ridiculously expensive, that pays wages that are stupidly low for workers and stupidly high for bosses. The Economy that rewards bankers and accountants way more than nurses and teachers. And when the Top End of Town breaks laws on insider trading or rips off retail banking customers, it expects to get away with a gentle rap over their manicured knuckles (or an 'enforceable undertaking' as it's known in the trade).

Here's the thing: we have never had enough cops on the street at The Top of End of Town. Moreover, the ones that are there are not very good cops. So, what is my cunning plan? To abolish 'wearing a suit' as a defence to white-collar crime and to replace our regulators — ASIC in particular — with a squadron of Front Office Ladies from our toughest schools. The incumbents have had their chance and flopped, now we need some real action . . . and attitude. My mum was a front-office lady who knew the name of every kid at Maroubra High School. She could look into their souls and ensure compliance with the uniform code. With Front Office Ladies running ASIC, Australia won't be letting its corporate types off nearly so lightly. The reality is that we have allowed banks and business generally to maximise their profits. Here's the thing: profits are good, maximising profits is a disaster — it inevitably causes harm and leads to crime.

To sum up, here's what we need to do on Fair Dinkum Law Enforcement:

- Replace ASIC with a squadron of Front Office Ladies or other equally scary enforcers.
- Abolish 'wearing a suit' as a defence to all corporate crimes.

Add your own policy ideas or doodles on **Fair Dinkum Law Enforcement** here:

3. Parliamentary Reform. Dressing and Decisionings.

Parliament is a rabble. If our kids behaved at school like our leaders carry on in federal parliament, they would all be given detention. Maybe lines. And not the kind some enjoy in the staff bathrooms at the end of a sitting session in Canberra. You know what I mean: the shouting at each other, the evasion of questions, the deliberate misrepresentation of what used to be known as The Facts.

To make matters worse, the dress code in parliament is appalling. Why do they all wear suits? Only a few of us throw one on in real life these days. We need a 'look book' that ensures our MPs dress more like the people they represent. The member for Cottesloe should rock up in boardies and the member for Devonport in a beanie. But we should draw the line at fancy dress. For example, former fish and chip shop proprietors of alleged Christian heritage should not be wearing burkas in the House. Onesies, mankinis and other stunt-wear will need a doctor's certificate.

More gravely, the way Australia makes big decisions needs an overhaul. For example, a clear majority of both houses of parliament should be required for really significant issues like . . . GOING TO WAR!!! (. . . sorry to shout). See, prime ministers and cabinets should not be able to decide to go to war all by themselves. War is not about the Prime Minister. Or even the cabinet. War is about all of US. You, me and even those annoying people in number 14 who use a leaf blower before 9am on a Sunday. A proper debate and a real decision supported by most of our elected representatives is called for. The current arrangements are almost designed to allow Australia to be used by our distant allies to fight in wars that suit them but are actually of no real use to us.

For consistency, this 'super-majority', as the boffins call it, should also be required for all the big calls we make as a nation . . . like whether to set up a new AFL team in Tasmania or when choosing a contestant for the Eurovision Song Contest. To be clear: if you need the support of both houses of parliament to overturn a dumb sales tax on tampons, putting our troops in harm's way should require a majority vote from all our elected representatives.

In brief, the main points for Parliamentary Reform include:

- A super majority for big decisions (e.g. going to war or choosing a Eurovision contestant)
- A dress code that reflects the diverse sartorial glory of the electorates of Australia
- Restrictions on stunt attire (no burkas for anyone called Pauline).

Add your ideas or doodles for **Parliamentary Reform: Dressing and Decisionings** here:

4. Electoral Reform. Pocket Money and Pencils.

Money is not great when mixed with politics. No kidding! Election campaigns should be financed by the people who do the voting and certainly not The Wealthier People who run The Economy. Each candidate should receive a small allowance from the federal budget — the money of We The People. We could call it Pocket Money. So we know whose pocket our politicians are in . . . OURS! Ha! Doesn't that sound good? Let's face it, most campaign money is spent on bad ads. Imagine if politics was a battle of ideas rather than dodgy videos. If we cut off the money supply: more ideas, less ads. We could also ban candidates from using their own money to pay for this stuff . . . cos that's basically betting on yourself. Footballers and cricketers can't do that, why should politicians be allowed?

Our voting process could also be improved. Until the early twentieth century you had to own property or be a bloke to get a pencil on polling day. That was what we might call a 'flawed system'. To be fair, people forget how new democracy is for our species. It's early days — only a hundred years ago women were hunger-striking for the vote in Britain. But we could make our elections much more fun and useful. Electors could be required to complete a task before they get to tick a box on the ballot paper. For example, sing a song or build a small brick fence. This might unfairly advantage kids who went to Steiner schools or did tech at TAFE but we could give it a go. By the way, does anyone know why we use pencils instead of pens when we enter the cardboard cubicle to make our indelible mark on democracy?!? We say 'indelible mark' but it's not is it? Why the hell do we use pencils?

Highlights and headlines on Electoral Reform include:

- Equal publicly funded Pocket Money for all political candidates
- Voters must complete an interesting task before they get a pencil on polling day.

Add your policy ideas or doodles on **Electoral Reform: Pocket Money and Pencils** here:

5. The Media. How to fix it.

Our age of fake news, click-bait and toxic trolling is a bit of a worry. As I read in the media every day, our Media has gone to the dogs. But The Media is all we've got. Politics, arts, economics are all viewed through the prism — or opaque rhomboid solid if you prefer — of The Wretched Media. In our wired world, The Media is virtually everything. Pun intended. Sorry. Reality itself is a media creation. Ever more centralised, commercialised and infantilised. The Media is a 24/7 rolling news-fiction event that we all inhabit.

As we all know, politics has drifted from statecraft to soap opera. Parliament is more like a lunchtime fight in the playground than a proper debate on matters of public interest. The thing about the public interest of course is that it's not that interesting. Not as interesting as, say, a quality BBC drama or a full-on cage-fight wrestling match, depending on your taste. The constant search for conflict in our political journalism, for an angle that makes people click and their eyeballs stick, is not what we need for the serious business of government. Government should be boring.

We need to get our politicians out of the media. Forcibly. With price signals and maybe the threat of jail time. Our elected representatives have a job to do — there's heaps of reading, briefings, consultations, advice, decisions — and they should bloody well get on with it. I say our politicians should be banned outright from making media appearances all weekend and on Wednesdays — on TV, in print and, of course, on Twitter or any other platform. For a start. Maybe we'll end up with our pollies only doing media one day a week! How's that sound? Motion carried!

The standard of conversation in interviews on our current affairs programs also needs some work. Certain hackneyed phrases should be outlawed and attract an on the spot fine. Prohibited phrases could include:

- 'good to be with you'
- 'thank you for your question'
- 'any time soon'

Feel free to list the phrases and clichés that you would ban right here:

In any event, if I was the TV presenter Leigh Sales and a politician said 'good to be with you' to me, I'd be saying: 'Hey mate, we'll see about that'.

Public broadcasting was once seen by everyone as a vital part of a functioning democracy. Like fluoride in the water. Doing the stuff that commercial organisations would not do: programs of educational value, shows about farming and of course, the cricket. What changed? We have public schools, public hospitals, public transport. And public broadcasting. We used to talk about eight cents a day being the cost of the ABC for the taxpayer but now that's the entire budget for Four Corners. The budget of the ABC needs to be doubled. Immediately. And let's not forget SBS. If private media companies are worried about competition they should learn how to do media properly, like companies in a genuinely competitive capitalist marketplace who need to reinvent themselves to stay relevant. Isn't this what capitalism is supposed to be about? We could also allow the ABC to top up its budget by crowdfunding key projects. This will enable Aunty to make the odd decent drama series, do more Play School and cover test cricket when the commercials finally give up on it. A day that is coming all too soon. It's a slow motion train crash I can't bear to watch.

In a nutshell, the takeaways from this bit on Media Reform as are follows:

- The budget of the ABC (and SBS) will be doubled and supported by crowdfunding.
- Politicians will not be allowed to do media on Weekends or Wednesdays.
- Fines will apply for saying 'good to be with you' and other clichés during an interview.

Add your own ideas or doodles on **The Media: How to fix.** it here:

6. Fiscal Rectitude. Paying for All The Things.

Fiscal. Rectitude. How we raise and spend our tax dollars. Or put another way . . . How We Build our Common Wealth. In my view, we get our finances all wrong. We talk a lot about the budget but not about how we actually spend the money. It's like trying to keep tabs on how your teenagers spend their allowance. Sure, we have Expenditure Review Committees but we somehow avoid the harder questions that might make a flying pinch of difference. We can find billions to build a gulag across the Pacific for refugees, but only spare change for affordable housing at home while thousands of veterans sleep rough every night. We find cash to subsidise truckies — who need a hand, don't get me wrong — but not enough for renewable energy. We spend nearly as much federal money on the military as we do on our schools. Around $30 billion a year. It wasn't like that even 5 years ago. Have We The People ever been asked what we think about this? No. Do we use golden bullets in our rifles? Do our drones have heated seats in the bathroom? Frankly it's one of the few things our major parties are eye-to-eye on. Why is that? We need to talk. We could put our money into a turbo-charged sovereign wealth fund instead, whose job it is to invest in new industries or to properly fund housing, education, hospitals, renewables and the arts. For starters.

So . . . what can we do about all this money stuff?

Well, Australia is a secular society. Sunday is a day for sleeping and fishing or making dresses and getting paid double time if you're lucky. We The People can believe what we like in our churches and mosques, kovils, shuls and ashrams, but our government is not run by anyone's god — it is run by people and for people. Faith is a private matter and it should stay that way. So, religions — or Faith Themed Businesses (FTBs) as I call them — should pay tax on their operations like any other commercial enterprise. The property and income of our leading

FTBs is eye watering. FTBs should make a proper contribution to our Common Wealth. Especially given the bad things some of them have been caught doing. We could also have a Dickhead Levy for FTBs that emphasise bizarre beliefs and wealth accumulation as an end in itself. Can you think of any that fit that particular bill?

We can also tax patriotism, the last cubby house of the scoundrel. I am thinking about flags. You see a lot more Australian flags these days in front yards. Australians used to be happy with a jacaranda or a pine tree out the front. Maybe a tire swing. Who needs a flag? We know where we live. A tax can discourage this excessive patriotism. Something like $100 per week. We tax alcopops and ciggies, so we can tax flags. We used to be as modest as Ken Rosewall, our old Davis Cup champion, about our national pride. What happened?

To save some serious coin, corporate tax accounting should be abolished as a profession. It deserves to go the way of Netscape, video stores and the Australian car industry. Into the dustbin of oblivion. Some corporate tax accountants are nice people. Like Derek. Drives an old Triumph Stag. Bangs on about his cycling posse and their ever-falling personal bests. Derek might be missed for a while, maybe the length of a long weekend. But he can always retrain at TAFE as his clients have been telling their retrenched staff for years.

See, the whole point of corporate tax accounting is to reduce the money collected by government for services and infrastructure, for nurses and teachers, firies and police, for swimming pools, libraries, sports fields and schools. Its goal is to ensure government cannot adequately fund a whole bunch of things that are good for everyone. How is this legal? Every deduction, every impenetrable trust, minimises the funds our government needs to own, run and do things for We The People. Before you say banning a profession is extreme, remember we've managed to ban CFCs, driving without seatbelts and keeping lions in your backyard. Surely we can ban a profession that does us no good at all.

This measure will have an immediate impact. Public assets will blossom across our cities and towns — heated swimming pools, a National Broadband Network that works at least half the time. Our coffers will flood with rivers of gold. Some companies will take their money elsewhere but most will stay because Australia is a wealthy and peaceful country, a bloody good place to invest. The threat of tax rates sending business overseas is mainly garbage spoken by greedy people who, deep down, just do not want to pay tax. Ever. They think taxation is theft. But that belief doesn't stop these people from using our roads, drinking our water and bleating about the need for government to fund their private schools.

Fiscal rectitude is not all about taxation. Investment incentives will boost key industries like cricket. The nets of Australia are empty. It's a national disgrace. Every household will receive an allowance to buy all members a new bat, a floppy hat, a tube of zinc cream and a water bottle. If you don't like cricket, ask yourself this: how is our time and money best spent — on war or cricket? If the world played more cricket — a game that goes for hours and hours with breaks for drinks and food — there would be more peace in our lives. Did you know that Afghanistan has emerged as a rising power in world cricket in recent years? An unlikely force for good in a war-torn country. War or Cricket, that is the question.

Pulling it all together, Fiscal Rectitude means:

- A sovereign wealth fund to invest in new industry, renewables, housing and the arts.
- Faith Themed Businesses — aka religions — will pay tax like other commercial entities.

- A tax of $100pw will apply to households who put an Australian flag out the front.
- Corporate tax accounting will be outlawed as a profession in its entirety.
- Every household gets an allowance for a new cricket bat, floppy hat and water bottle.

Add your own policy ideas or doodles on **Fiscal Rectitude: Paying for all the Things** here:

7. Human Rights. The Comeback Tour!

Human rights need to make a comeback. Once loved by all and sundry, today Human Rights languish like an old rock band waiting for a call from its dead manager. Luckily it is now acceptable for our faded pop stars to do revival tours so they can put a deposit down on assisted living accommodation or a mobile home. Superannuation Rock! The moment has arrived for Human Rights to hit the road and do a few leagues clubs.

After the horrors of the Second World War our species created laws to protect people for simply being human beings. Human rights are ideas and laws that remind us we are all the same. This seems to annoy some people, but human rights are something we all share. Like breathing. From the bloke who sleeps in the park down the road to the Queen herself.

Anyone can be mistreated or abused by more powerful forces — companies, institutions, individuals or, god forbid, government itself. Imagine it was you that was subject (hypothetically) to indefinite detention by a government on a tiny island in the Pacific, or to waterboarding somewhere in Africa at the hands of an allied power? Obviously a nice country like ours would never be associated with that stuff because it is not nice to lock people up indefinitely or to torture them. Is it? That doesn't fit with a 'fair go for everyone' at all. How can we be a fair dinkum country if we jail people who have not committed an offence, then give them no idea about how or when they might be getting out?

In my view, we need a Bill of Rights that spells out how we are all protected, equally, including Collingwood supporters and Clive Palmer voters. We all have the same right to free speech, assembly, liberty, equality before the law and so on. A Bill of Rights would enshrine the invisible important things no one bothers to make reality TV shows about. Our rights to subsist, to work, to strike, to education and even shelter. To a clean and healthy environment. Wow!

Either way, if elected I will propose a Private Members Bill to make Gillian Triggs, former President of the Human Rights Commission, our National Life Coach. For life. Julian Burnside could be her deputy. Or maybe Geoffrey Robertson. Or Jana Wendt. Maybe Ita Buttrose?

So, just quickly, we have these action items on Human Rights . . .

- Gillian Triggs will be appointed National Life Coach.
- Human Rights — The Leagues Club Tour. It's on!
- A Bill (or Gillian) of Rights.

Add your own policy ideas or doodles on **Human Rights. The Comeback Tour** here:

8. Efficiency Drivers. Making the most of our money and things.

Government is a wild and unruly beast. It's harder to keep neat and tidy than your garage. In government, it's traditional these days to waste untold millions on team meetings and extravagant travel arrangements. I ask you: what's wrong with a motel where you get a jug of water and a glass of milk in the fridge with a paper cover on it? Not to mention the money wasted on consultancy fees because there's no one left in the department with genuine knowledge of the subject area since the last round of job cuts. No one stops to do the maths for what government used to spend on staff compared with our outlay on consultants. We don't do that because there is no money and no one still employed has the skills to do it. If we did do it we might have a collective nervous breakdown when we realise the stupidity of clearing out all that corporate memory and competence to save a few bob we aren't saving anyway.

Let's be clear about what we have done. On a bi-partisan basis over the last generation we've unwound one of the great achievements of western civilisation — an independent public service. We've turned our bureaucrats into nervous Nellies on short-term contracts who wonder how they will be able to pay their mortgages after they get the boot when government changes at the next election. Given the chance I would ask The Ghost of Nugget Coombs to do an 'expenditure review' of how much we have saved. I'm pretty sure he'd do it for nothing (just as most of us do unpaid overtime these days). To be fair, if I was Nugget — having basically set up modern Australian government from the Reserve Bank to the Australia Council — I would be mightily miffed at our lack of respect for his life's work.

Government squanders nearly as much money on unproductive activity and self-indulgence as the Business Community. Nearly but not quite. Many inefficiencies remain, even at the ABC which must not be beyond the reach of a committed effort to economise. For starters, the broadcast of federal parliament should be merged with the flagship ABC television program 'Q&A'. There is little point in having two separate shows essentially dealing with the same subject: how we are governed. Moreover, there is bound to be broad appeal in allowing Australians to text our fearless leaders while they're at the despatch box in question time.

We could call the new program Question Australia and ask real questions of ministers like 'Does Close the Gap include Pine Gap?' or 'Given all the military and security personnel Australia has trained over the last decade in the Middle East, are we happy with their NAPLAN results?' The entire nation would tune in. Tony Jones could be speaker. Or Annabel Crabbe, to get the giggles going. She must be a bit frustrated, mind you, being so clever and having no real impact on the circus that swirls around her.

A summary of proposed Efficiency Drivers . . .

- The broadcast of parliament and QandA will be merged into one monster TV program.
- The Ghost of Nugget Coombs will conduct an expenditure review of, well, everything.

Add your ideas on **Efficiency Drivers: Making the most of our money and things** here:

9. Mandatory Optimism. No, really . . . cheer up!

We hear a lot about culture these days. The Sydney Swans footy team are famous for their No Dickheads culture. The Banks are renowned for their Dickheads Only culture. We seem to have a problem with our culture across the broader community, like in the air we breathe. Many of us among We The People are a bit down in the mouth. I'm not talking about clinically depressed people — that's a separate, if related, issue. The Economy has turned into a machine for making people unhappy then making money out of that unhappiness through franchised pizza delivery, televised corporate sport and wandering around malls as a form of recreation. A little everyday miserableness is understandable — given slow internet speeds, rampant authoritarianism and the melting of the polar ice caps — but only to a point. With all due respect, we're not alive long enough to be pessimistic.

Thirty years ago there was no internet, no native title, no female CEOs. And no decent Indian restaurants, if we're being honest, anywhere in Australia (actually that's still true round our way, I would love a reliable source of beef vindaloo). The world has clearly changed for the better in so many ways since 1988. Infant mortality is down across the globe. Girls go to school even in the poorest countries in numbers that were once unimaginable. Smoking is banned in pubs, even in Scotland (arguably the most impressive achievement of our species over the last century). And there's no MSG in Chinese restaurants anywhere outside the Gold Coast.

So things can and do change, for the better. If we want to Make Australia Slightly Better than Average Again™, if we want to Rebuild Our Common Wealth, we need to acknowledge that things can change, do change and will be able to change again! And if I have to I will legislate to get people moving in the right direction.

Remember this:

- Cheer up, things change and can change again
- Our species managed to ban smoking in Scottish pubs, so anything is possible!
- I will introduce a Mandatory Optimism Act if you force me.

Add your own ideas or doodles on Mandatory Optimism. No, really . . . cheer up! here:

10. The Chicxalub Principle. Together we can defeat the Dinosaurs!

A meteorite once hit Earth and annihilated the dinosaurs. Did you know that? Chicxalub it was called, after a town nearby in southern Mexico. Whatever the creationists say, around 65 million years ago a mighty boulder 10 kilometres across left a 100 kilometre-wide crater in the Yucatan peninsula. Chicxalub sent our beautiful planet into a long, long night, destroying three-quarters of all living creatures including the dinosaurs. One minute brontosauruses were gently grazing on kale then . . . bang! A toxic cloud hung over the earth for years and years. Like Beijing on a bad day, only for much, much longer. It was nasty.

My point? It was a huge, destiny-altering event. And no one saw it coming. A cave painting on the outskirts of Caracas suggests a precocious proto-flamingo had an inkling of the looming catastrophe, but otherwise Chicxalub came out of the blue. So many highlights of human history are the same. Louis XVI was the last true emperor of La Belle France. One minute he was inhaling the lavender perfume on his frilly shirt cuffs, next minute his head was in a basket. Or Tsar Nicholas. A living god ruling all Mother Russia until the day his Winter Palace was overrun by filthy peasants and even filthier intellectuals. And then there's Kevin Rudd. The kid no one liked at school in Nambour who got his revenge by becoming prime minister. One minute, Kevin was the leader of a prosperous, progressive nation, the next . . . And then he made a cameo again. And now um . . . er . . . every day, somewhere on earth Rudd is talking, talking about his chosen topic, himself, to himself. But the point holds . . . remember 9/11? Or the GFC?!?

OK. You should now put on some stirring Movie Music to enhance the finale. The theme from Chariots of Fire. Or some early AC/DC. Loud major chords please. My point is simple: We The People can be the Chicxalub of change and justice. A Chicxalub that serves our Common

Wealth and defeats the dinosaurs. Even Eric Abetz. We can create a Government that is more like us. We can rebuild our Common Wealth. But only if we get involved. We need to stop outsourcing politics to people who rely on re-election for their livelihoods. We need to do stuff ourselves, every week, every day, working through Our List of Things to Make Australia Slightly Better Than Average Again™. I do not expect you to like this, but 'no pain, no gain', right? How come a personal trainer can say that and everyone goes 'cool' but if someone says that about politics we tell them to 'get stuffed'?!? Yes, I am prepared be your representative on the Crossbench, your secular shepherd, you beautiful, woolly humans. So . . . wherever you are. Stand up. On the count of 3 . . . make a loud and proud, clear and confident, BAA-ing sound. Ready? Do it now . . . One. Two. Three. BAA-BAAA-BAAAA!!! Thank you.

In summary:

- No one saw Chicxalub coming.
- Get involved. Be the Chicxalub of Change. Do whatever you can.
- We can Make Australia Slightly Better Than Average Again™. No risk!

Add your ideas on **The Chicxalub Principle: Together we can defeat the Dinosaurs.** here:

PART FOUR:
Infrequently asked questions

n this part we consider the infrequently asked questions traversing my synapses and addling the country:

- Why Slightly Better Than Average Again?
- Why do I care?
- Am I Talking Class Warfare?
- Why run for the Senate?
- Are you in my Constituency?
- Why am I Sort of Independent?
- What is politics really 'about', whatever your politics may be?
- Last question . . . is it possible to summarise all this?

Why Slightly Better Than Average Again?

Why not Great? Why Not Amazing? Because it will be an achievement for us to get back to Slightly Better than Average. With what we've done to the reef, public transport, and test cricket. I make no apology for this apparently modest goal. It's obviously Un-Australian to talk about being Great. By the way, I dislike the term Un-Australian (because it's a bit Un-Australian). But, frankly, our wonderful country has always had too many problems and too much to get better at, for us to think of ourselves as Great. And when Clive Palmer decided in 2018 to use the slogan 'Make Australia Great' in his new bright yellow billboard campaign, ripping off that bloke in the US whose name escapes me, we all knew that Great is not so great. So Slightly Better Than Average Again™ will do just fine. It's self-deprecating and shows we don't take ourselves too seriously. It is, in itself, slightly better than average.

In a way I want us to get back in touch with the better features of my Australian childhood. I grew up in the 1970s when Australia had an image of itself as friendly and productive, welcoming and hard-working. It was a country that made lots of cars and films. Its cricket nets and netball courts were full. We had enough for free milk at recess, free university education and a bi-partisan commitment to home ownership and social housing. I am campaigning for a country that once again looks forward to its future. Looking back we used to manage our fear with the hope of a gradually improving world. If this is nostalgia, I would say it is the right kind of nostalgia. To be clear, I am not looking for a return to The White Australia Policy, sacking pregnant women, terra nullius or the death penalty. OK? That is the wrong kind of nostalgia. The kind we get from our reactionary populists.

Deep down I'm also campaigning for reality. Life as it's lived rather than as it's advertised. Dreams are good. Ambition is pretty good, too. Heroes are good, if you want one. But what if you're happy muddling through every day, loving your partner and kids, juggling a parenting plan, growing a few vegetables in the backyard and looking forward to next weekend's sport when the Under 16s Girls play The Tigers away in a top of the table clash? It's going to be a cracker! There's a sausage sizzle with vegan options. Terry and Terri will be on the tongs as usual. Lemonade pikelets are also in the offing. In my experience, most people would settle for Slightly Better Than Average and be pretty happy with that.

Many of us don't have heroes. Being or having a hero makes many people anxious even nauseous. Sometimes we might get goosebumpy about a hero for a bit. Maybe Nelson Mandela, famed nemesis of apartheid. Or Sam Kerr for her soccer skills? Some people are amazing. And ambitious. And good on them. But most of us are not. We need to construct a world, a country, a politics based on how most people live. Most of the amazing people can look after themselves. The real challenge is how to make sense of your life when it's unspectacular or a bit of a mess. If all this makes sense then, well . . . I'm your guy. Together, we can create a country where the standard is 'good enough'. Where everything is kind of alright, slightly better than average. Where there's always time for a chat about nothing much.

And, to keep digging a little deeper, we're all gonna die. Except for cancer research or euthanasia, that fun fact doesn't get much airplay in our politics. We all stare into the beauty of the sky and the abyss of eternity as equals. Whether we sleep in the park or the Lodge, on the beach or at Buckingham Palace. As the cliché goes, life really is too short. Beautiful and painfully brief. It's certainly too short to get hung up about religion. I went to church every Sunday until my last week in high school. Here's the one thing that stayed with me: 'you shall be judged by how you treat the least among you'. Judged by other humans, that is. I don't need a god to make life meaningful or treat my fellow citizens properly, because when I think about our shared fate, our shared fragility, it fills me with compassion, it strengthens my connection to other people. I am being deadly serious now. If we can trust that feeling, we don't need a god. That's my theology.

If we are going to Make Australia Slightly Better Than Average Again™, I want to be really clear about certain things. Your house and your car do not impress me, even if they are amazing. Like a Maybach or Tesla. Or a mint condition 1976 Datsun 260Z. If you have a massive wide screen TV, may you savour long hours on the couch twiddling with the remote. If you have a raked zen sand garden with a whisper-quiet water feature, that's terrific. Why not? I hope you enjoy that, too. Also, your job is not important. Not really. Well, maybe if you're a bridge builder or oncologist. I don't want a bridge to collapse under anyone or for my cancer to go undetected. Also, I love broccoli, so if you're a broccoli farmer, I'm open to being seduced by your produce. And olives. Oysters, too.

What really counts to me — and to nearly everyone I've respected in my life — is who you are in your bones. We judge that mainly by looking at how you treat others and what you give to the world. It's the kind of homely wisdom we used to get from our grandparents. The stuff I learnt while eating my nana's apple cake, or while Pop was teaching me how to bowl a leg-spinner (he played first grade for Randwick, something I never threatened to do). Yes, what matters is the good things you bring into the world. It might be cakes or songs. Or jokes and a single-handed backhand, like my mum who played A Grade at White City. You might do it by just turning up, by being there for your family, your friends or your football club. You are what you give, not what you own or do. Are you with me?

An Australia that is Slightly Better Than Average Again™ is all about Nana's Apple Cake or Pop's Googly, and about not The Open-Slather Raw Meat Fed Economy of Total Competition and Profit Maximisation. Imagine our country as a great big sausage sizzle (naturally with vegetarian and vegan options). An Australia like a fete or farmers' market, all day and all night, all year, year in and year out. Everyone is welcome. That is the vision. A country like a mixed doubles day at the local tennis club. Where a good forehand is admired but a dodgy second serve is tolerated because you're good company. That is the Australia of my childhood. Or the best bits. And it's the kind of Australia I want for our future.

We've sacrificed so many of the good things, the Slightly Better Than Average things, that we had. And for what? We have become a country that bleats about 'jobs and growth' like some poor old fella with Tourettes, that rails against refugees whose only crime is not have been born in Cottesloe or Killara, that has convinced itself a house is an asset rather than a home whose purpose is to raise a family, have parties and erect a backyard trellis covered in passionfruit vines. We should build homes for humans, not for markets that create too few winners and too many losers.

Let's face it, We The People are often just trying to get through the day and minimise the damage to our hearts and souls. Life is a bit of a struggle a lot of the time. Even though most of us are comfortable enough, somehow it's still a stretch and pretty damn stressful. And for some it is no fun at all. We talk about 'resilience' being a good thing, something to admire but I'm not so sure. It seems to mean 'suck it up' — like that's a good thing. To a point we should roll with the punches, but depression and suicide aren't boom industries in modern Australia for nothing. We should base the politics of our nation and our communities on these ordinary facts of life as it is lived and be more than happy with Slightly Better Than Average Again™.

Lest we forget . . . Everyone is Welcome.

What does Making Australia Slightly Better Than Average Again™ mean for you? Write your answer below.

Why do I care?

Probably because I have the working class values of my grandparents.
Never shook them. Frank and Lil. They were Irish Catholics who never
owned their own home or a car. They worked just about every day of
their lives because 'that was what you did'. As they brought up their
family — two daughters — in the 1940s and 50s — the parish priest
preached about the threat the communists posed to people like my
grandparents who hung pictures of Jesus and Mary in the lounge room,
and how the lovely little primary school the church was building on
the hill would be funded by using the spare change of the poor. Politics
was not a profession remote from the people back then. We were all in
it together. People met in pubs to talk about the future of the country
and went to party meetings. My Granddad was a 'DLP' man and my
grandmother, Nin, as we called her, didn't agree with him at all. The
Democratic Labor Party were a bunch of anti-communist, super-
conservative Catholics who split from the Australian Labor Party in the
mid 1950s. My other grandfather, Pop, was a salesman and Labor voter,
gregarious and hedonistic. Granddad was more disciplined and stern.

My grandfathers would argue politics over a beer every Friday night.
They stood on either side of the split in the ALP — one of the great
cultural schisms in our history. Most people alive today barely know
it happened. My other grandmother, by the way, had little interest in
politics. She was a terrific painter and milliner and trained as a singer
at the Conservatorium. Say what you like about my grandparents, but
they talked and lived politics like it mattered, like they were part of the
big adventure, the great unfolding story of Australia. That's what politics
was. A worker's democracy for some. A looming outpost for godless
communists for others. My grandparents connected me to a way of
politics that has nearly disappeared during my life. We need to reclaim
that spirit. And we can.

Am I talking Class Warfare?

Some people stop me out the front of the supermarket and ask: 'Are you talking about Class Warfare, mate?' Hmm. So what exactly is Class Warfare? It's a term used by The Wealthier People to refer to The Not So Wealthy when they complain about lack of access to good housing, holidays, education and a whole bunch of things The Wealthier People enjoy and others do not. When the Not So Wealthy suggest changing the slightest thing about society, its economy and our tax system, in the interests of social equality, they are accused of waging Class Warfare (or its close cousin the Politics of Envy). When a person says, 'Oh, but that's class warfare' what they really mean is, 'I am quite happy with my comfortable life and you can get stuffed'.

To understand Class Warfare we need to remember the history of politics, right back from when the Pharoahs built the pyramids with slaves, many of whom died (just as people perished building the Harbour Bridge or making your T-shirt in Bangladesh). Progress throughout history has been the process of giving power and wealth a bit of a shake-up. Once, nearly all power and wealth was held by the king. Now we can all own property, women can vote and slavery is illegal. Over time, power and wealth have been gradually shared more equally. Usually the shifts in power and wealth have occurred with more than a little violence because the powerful rarely surrender. From the English Civil War to the Revolutions of France and Russia, kings and nobles had their heads removed. Workers were shot dead in miners' strikes in England and America. Revolutions, coups and wars. There has been a lot of strife in winning political rights even in our relatively peaceful and prosperous western countries.

For most of the twentieth century it was a common goal to share more and more power and wealth more and more equally. That's what the Welfare State was about. A system of providing subsistence and support for the infirm and disabled, the unemployed and the widowed. Social housing. Public health and education, too. These things didn't exist as recently as the nineteenth century. Yet they were at the heart of our social democracy for decades. Key features of capitalism during its most successful period, the second part of the twentieth century. Supported by progressive taxation: the more you earned, the more you paid, because you got more out of society than others. As suburbs expanded in Australia and Britain and North America and Europe, so did the Welfare State and our Common Wealth.

Some say the Welfare State was designed to stop us from going communist. And there is some truth in this. Communism was pretty popular among The Not So Wealthy in the 1940s and 1950s in Australia — not as popular as rock'n'roll or netball, but enough to keep The Wealthier People concerned. The failure of the experiments in collective enterprise in Russia and China — with their death camps, starvation and killings — does not explain why we lost faith in our own, more boring, processes of sharing and collective endeavour. At some point (maybe about 1986?) the project of sharing more and more power and wealth in western democracies stopped. We stopped believing in the things we thought we believed in. We stopped even trying to be an egalitarian society. We voted for policies we thought were good — deregulation and privatisation, tax cuts, free trade and labour market reform — without thinking through the consequences. We voted for Opportunity before Outcome without a proper chat around the campfire over a prawn and a beer.

When people talk about reorganising wealth and power, they get accused of Class Warfare. Mainly by politicians or pundits on cable TV with nothing better to do. Perhaps because it is easier to sledge a person than it is to argue the issues like grown-ups. A few people reading this book will accuse me of Class Warfare and that might even be good for sales. But Class Warfare, to be honest, is in fact the process by which

The Wealthier People keep their wealth and power. Class Warfare means paying CEOs more than they deserve, making real estate stupidly expensive, and putting university out of reach for too many of The Not So Wealthy. Among many other things. Class Warfare is waged by The Wealthier People against the Not So Wealthy every day. On television. In parliament. In the streets. They know they are doing it. And why.

What's your definition of Class Warfare? Write your answer below. Neatly or expressively.

Why run for the Senate?

Because that's where the power is and outsiders can make a difference. Here's how federal parliament works. The House of Representatives, our Lower House, has 150 members from electorates or seats all over the country. It's where the action is. If you have a majority in The Reps, you get to run the government and appoint the Prime Minister — the school captain of Australia. But the Senate, the Upper House, and its 76 members must approve all legislation before it becomes law. Even if the Lower House passes a law it still has to get through the Senate. Sucked in! So the Senate can reject new laws or modify them and, importantly, it can horse-trade with the government of the day to get a deal for their constituents or supporters.

The Senate has 76 Senators including 12 from each of the six states: New South Wales, Victoria, Queensland, Western Australia, South Australia and Tasmania; and two each from the Australian Capital Territory and Northern Territory. The Senate was designed to protect the states (just like in the USA) to ensure the little ones didn't get stood over by the big ones. So, this system means that all the states get the same say and the Territories get to interrupt a bit. All of this makes sense but is also a bit mad. Paul Keating once described the Senate as 'unrepresentative swill' because a senator from Tasmania only needs a fraction of the votes you need in a big state like New South Wales to get elected but they have the same voting power in parliament. And today the Senate has a lot of power.

Why is this so? Well, We The People have a long-standing distrust for our big parties, so we tend to vote to ensure that the government never has a majority in the Senate. And have done since the 1980s. That's not entirely a bad thing. In fact, it helps keep the government honest — it needs to fight for its laws to be passed. But we can also end up with a bunch of odd-bods controlling what's called the balance of power.

Out of the 76 seats in the Senate, the Coalition has 31 seats, Labor 26 and the Greens have 9. We then have a cricket team of misfits who make up the rest. We call this the crossbench because they sit across from the government in a huddle, like the new kids at school. They are independents or members of small parties — and tend to come and go from election to election.

But stop right there, People of Australia. How many Senators can you name? Probably around the same number as African currencies you can tell me about without googling. The Dirham. The Rand. And, that's it. Even political tragics who listen to the news every hour only know a few senators. Yet these people control the fate of every law passed by our parliament. Funnily enough you probably do know some of the folks on the Crossbench precisely because they often determine the outcome of a big vote, so it hits the news. Like Pauline Hanson and Derryn Hinch, the former journalist, or David Leyonhelm, a retired animal doctor and hard core libertarian (an old school patriarchal chap but I respect his stance on euthanasia).

In short, the crossbench is a bit of a shower of right-wing reactionary populists. It reflects Australia even less than the parliament in general. Yet the crossbench determines the outcome of legislation whenever the Opposition disagrees with the government. The government needs to suck up to these odd bods to get stuff done. Some, like the Centre Alliance Senators, are moderate and centrist (code for pretty damn conservative but not as crazy as the others). But most are well to the right of the political spectrum, like One Nation (anti-immigration and anti-union), Family First (strong on god) and Leyonhelm's Liberal Democratic Party (anti-government in general but pro-gun and pro-smoking — great guy to have at a party). And these people get an awful lot of airtime in our national conversation.

Our Senate should speak for the whole of our society. For people like you and me who might be sceptical about shopping as the basis for an economy. For people who like art and believe everyone should sing every day — and not just in the shower! For people who want a story about where the country and its economy is going. For people who are like a lot of people you know. Joining the crossbench gives someone a chance to get new ideas into the national conversation — like the ideas running around in this book. A different kind of populism. An articulate populism that reflects our complexity and diversity. A populism based on rebuilding our Common Wealth and powered by the vision that we can make Australia Slightly Better Than Average Again™.

If I became a senator I would of course represent a particular state — New South Wales — and I would be really keen to remind the nation there are loads of people who live good lives outside of our cities. Paul Keating said anyone not living in Sydney was basically camping. Wrong! There are loads of businesses and interesting things happening outside of cities. All over Australia. Energy retailers, new generation farmers, call centres, teachers, nurses, and creative people who can't be bothered with the pace and property prices of our cities, who want to focus on their thing and their families more than money and competing. The regions are ready to rumble and I'd be more than happy to tell that story properly in the Senate.

The crossbench has power. Way too much. It needs new faces to better reflect the country. The Senate needs new people and new ideas. People Like Us. Even me.

Am I bonkers or onto something with all this, folks? Write your answer and any questions you may have below.

Are you in my Constituency?

People ask me . . . often at kids' football, when the visiting team is ahead and we're looking at the ground, kicking the dust and wondering what to talk about . . . 'who is your constituency?' Let me tell you. And I'm being serious here . . . My constituency is:

- People who sing in choirs for the sheer love of it.
- And those who do the tuck shop at kids footy.
- People visiting their parents in a slightly sad aged care home.
- The kid learning Chinese so they can read Confucius in the original.
- Parents who sit with their kids and work through quadratic equations.
- Bank tellers who love a good detective novel.
- Checkout staff who have every record made by Aretha Franklin in well-scratched vinyl.
- The rugby league or netball team currently running fourth in Group 7.
- The policeman who saved a grieving friend from a burning house but hasn't been the same since.
- Anyone who is not on television.
- The woman who wakes at 3am worried that she will not make her rent or mortgage payment this month even though she's worked 2 jobs and not drunk red wine for 3 years.
- The immigrant googling the term nature-strip.
- The burn victim.
- The dux of every school.
- Everyone who gave everything in an exam and did a tiny bit better than expected.
- And the one who struggled and isn't sure what to do next.
- And nurses. Especially nurses, for without nurses we are barbarians.

Does that sound like you???

Are you with me?

Who else do you think should be part of our constituency?

Why am I sort of Independent?

Good question. No one can really be independent. We are all connected to each other, aren't we? So, independence is a bit of a myth. For me it's really about being independent of the major political parties. So call me Non-Aligned if you like. And in the end, because of the way the voting system works, I might have to form a party anyway. That's because you have a much better chance of being elected if you have your own column on the Senate ballot paper. And only parties get their own column.

'Why not work with one of the major parties?' I hear you ask. My answer generally would be 'Sorry but that's how we got to this point in our history'. With a parliament that doesn't really reflect Australia. By voting for parties that don't bring out the best in our best. There are people of great character and drive, of good faith and intent, who have disappeared without trace in our political parties. Some have even been eaten alive by their colleagues, let alone opponents, while being Prime Minister.

I have joined two political parties over the years and left both (no prize for guessing which ones). Why am I not a member of a political party now?

The conservative parties are owned by their corporate and, increasingly, religious supporters. They govern not in the public interest but in the interests of large companies and socially conservative ideas. For the conservatives the workers of this country do not really exist, they are more like an unpleasant vapour than a real thing. The prevailing commitment to trickle-down economics among many conservatives is morally indefensible and intellectually dishonest. The crumbs fall from the top table in slow motion and mostly never reach the floor. The hostility of conservatives to trade unions overlooks the role organised labour has played through history in civilising our society — our people died not only in wars overseas but in mines and factories at home. They died fighting for the right to strike, here and abroad, and for a living wage and decent conditions of work. Conservatives tend to celebrate fallen service people but not fallen workers. The enthusiasm among many conservatives for mining our land, for using and exploiting nature without due care for the consequences, like the playground bullies of our planet, is not cool and not for me. The deliberate return of religious ideas to public debate is a regression because our public culture is secular. If we want to be like Jesus, why not go into the Temple — a place full of god-fearing hedge fund managers, franchise chain owners, bond market traders, real estate agents and financial planners — and turn over their tables like Jesus did? Coffee cups and laptops everywhere. Jesus sat with the poor and weak.

The so-called progressive party is out of date and out of touch. Once upon a time workers were organised into unions and had broadly similar life experiences. Now workers are a diverse lot. Most of us work in offices and have soft hands. Many who work in factories now are very well paid and looked after. Most workers do not even belong to unions. But jobs are increasingly more casual and insecure. Kids and the poor are unemployed in huge numbers or get less work than they want or need. Yet the so-called workers party sucks up to business because it thinks it cannot be elected without being respectable and respectful. It tries to be nice to business rather than making the effort to understand it. The party more or less ignores the business of creating wealth (this is a serious problem) — the long-term challenge of developing industry and creating sustainable businesses. It is also confused by hard-working people who have small businesses who can struggle to make ends meet yet employ so many workers. Unions are important but should not dominate a party that wants to govern a complex post-industrial society. Above all, this party has been way too timid for too long. An agenda of better education, health and housing is good but it needs to be complemented by bolder programs for wealth creation and industry development. Our so-called opposition is too quiet on that. Like it is quiet on the rights of those excluded from our society because it doesn't want to annoy powerful people who might not let them be the government. This is especially true for asylum seekers, anti-terror laws, homelessness, unemployment and, oddly, restrictions on trade unions. In the end, the ALP goes along with too much of the agenda of the ruling class and nearly always has done (who remembers when Chifley sent the army in to work the mines?).

The Greens are not really a major party. In my view, they need at least 20 per cent of the vote to be a player. The party struggles to reach 10. The main reason for that is that the Greens do not talk to the community as a whole. Climate change needs urgent action everywhere on earth, so the Greens should be a huge political force. For them to struggle when the planet is in crisis is a massive fail of political nous. Don't get me wrong, I admire the Greens' commitment to climate change action and human rights, and the protests of activists over decades. I also understand the hostility they face. But the Greens do not take wealth creation and the fears of workers seriously enough. If the Greens could tell the story of how a renewable economy can deliver jobs to the Not So Wealthy, it would be much more popular. But instead the Greens are stuck in a loop talking to their base (and have been known to argue amongst themselves a bit like the major parties).

Maybe you would like to run for the senate yourself? With a party, with me or on your own? Write your answer below.

What is politics really about, whatever your politics may be?

No one has ever asked me this question. Not at the shops. Or kids football. Not even round the fire on the other side of a barrel of rum. So, what is politics about? Under the bonnet? When you really get down to it?

Fear. People everywhere do not want to go without, to starve or be poor, to risk not having a job, to have their business go under, or to lay off staff who were poorly paid to begin with. Under the skin of most of us is a real and serious worry that everything will come unstuck. That the family home could be lost if things go wrong. Fear is the bedrock of politics. This can be missed when we are so busy working to pay the mortgage or drinking to forget we're struggling to do that, or talking about how our kids are going at school or whether the Tigers are going to make the semis.

In most countries, in most elections, people vote for the parties that make them the least afraid about their economic prospects — their jobs and businesses. Sure, we worry about terrorism and climate change and hospitals and schools, but under all that is a deep well of fear that has little to do with well-articulated and fully costed policies. People know enough about history, doubt themselves enough, and question their leaders enough to be rightly concerned about how things will turn out. We all know someone who has lost a job, lost their house, lost a business. For real.

We need to address the fears people have by taking the working lives of people more seriously. We need to create a viable, believable future that generates hope in us all. It is hard to find work, to find the work you want, to build a business, to compete internationally. We need to be more honest about unemployment and underemployment. We need to be smarter about how we invest. We need to appreciate how hard it is to run a small business and employ people. Above all we need to talk seriously about building our future communities. We will always worry but we should not be afraid. We need to build our Common Wealth so we can keep our fear down to a dull and manageable roar.

Do you agree? Write your answer below. Or draw a stick figure screaming. Your call.

Is it possible to summarise all this?

Maybe. My sound bites need work. But here goes . . .

Conservatives put business first and expect us to believe that the success of business guarantees the success of everyone if they work hard. That is what Trickle Down Economics, Privatisation and Tax Cuts are all about. It is pure ideology. In fact it is more like theology. And it is nonsense. Most people are too damn busy surviving to do anything about it or — sadly — have been conned into believing it.

The so-called progressive party lacks a real story of how a reforming government would work, because it has accommodated the main story of The Wealthier People. It has accepted the politics and policies of Opportunity over Outcome. It promises no real change but (ironically) a more competent version of the conservative alternative. After all, the whole era of Privatisation here was begun by the ALP under the Hawke-Keating government in the 1980s because the Libs didn't have the ticker to do it. Honestly, can anyone tell me the vision Labor has for our economic development beyond investing in education?

Meanwhile the Greens seem to think the planet matters more to people than business and jobs. And while it probably should, it definitely doesn't.

So, that is why I am not with the majors. No one is truly independent. No one can be. I am utterly dependent on you. Finally, here's something I'd really like to reiterate. So I'll say it again . . . we have been way too complacent about how government has been used and abused by ALL political parties. We The People of Australia have to take a bit of the blame and then take action to change it.

Are you with me? Cos we really need to do this together. We all need to do our bit to Make Australia Slightly Better Than Average Again™.

Take a moment to scribble aimlessly in this box or write a few of your own Infrequently Asked Questions.

PART FIVE:
As unfit for office as you are

As I went around Australia doing my political satire shows over the last year people would come up afterwards and say, hey that was funny but you really should give it a crack. As in, run for office. Initially I thought people were being polite but it happened at every gig. From Melbourne to Alice Springs. I've done 40 odd shows this year so maybe the whole exercise was a weird kind of focus group, policy testing process thing. Along the way I started thinking, well, satire in the end is really a just a way of workshopping our disappointment and frustration. It's social therapy masquerading as entertainment. So the thought formed that maybe I should listen to these people who had paid me to make them smirk and squirm.

But then I couldn't shake this fundamental feeling that I'm unfit for public office. You might feel the same way yourself. If you have any class. No one who wants to be a candidate should be allowed to be one, right? The last person to give power to is the one who is really, really keen to have it. The truth is few people are silly enough to put themselves forward; most of us are way too sensible. I am determined to give this politics caper a good solid crack but remain full of self-doubt. In this section I will explain why as I attempt to rise to the challenge of Making Australia Slightly Better Than Average Again™.

An Obscure Life

To begin with, I have no track record in anything in particular. It's been an obscure and mixed life to date. I would never describe what I have done as a career. I have worked as a low-flying lawyer and even lower flying writer-performer. I have loved most of it though. These days I run a low-cost community legal clinic in my town. It's useful and interesting work. I also chip in as company secretary for a community-owned renewables company. As a comic, if I get 100 people to a gig I'm delighted. I play grass roots football and cricket and sit on the board of a circus. I've been a director of a theatre company and a credit union. I once had a play I wrote professionally produced in those well-known theatre strongholds of Brisbane and Sacramento! I also sing in a choir called Dustyesky that has an unlikely following across the country and in Russia, 28 middle-aged men, sweaty and hairy, performing songs in a language we do not speak. Our objective is to make sure the audience has nearly as much fun as we do. None of this is stellar but it all makes me happy. It's slightly above average on a good day and that is fine by me.

So I am not Gough Whitlam or Helen Clark (the former NZ prime minister who I have always hugely admired). Nothing like it. Mind you, the track records of most candidates nowadays are pretty unimpressive and obscure if you think about it. Most of us would struggle to say what our local member did before entering politics. Many MPs are lifetime party operatives who work their way up from volunteering or advisor jobs and know little of so-called real life. So maybe my mixed and unspectacular career is no bad thing.

But more gravely for an aspiring politician, my life has been sketchy, at times downright debauched. People are not candid about these things in Australia and I don't want to boast, but it really has been tremendously enjoyable much of the time. Sometimes, though, it's been all over the shop. Too much. Just so you know. I have an old mate — an ex-rock star cum TV writer — who I used to talk to in those periods when things got really out of shape. It was always oddly comforting that no matter how loose I got, he was always way further out on the limb of excess. I told him that once and he joked: 'yeah I feel that way about Ivan Milat'. Dark sense of humour. Nothing drastic involved here, to be honest, but I certainly inhaled, even if pot was never really my thing. Let's leave it at that!

Marching to Canberra from Mullum

Friends, a little self-doubt is good. It's a quality we don't see enough of in political life. Self-reflection is certainly in the air where I live these days. The locals are always reflecting on their personal journeys and what not. I'm a Sydney boy — Sydney High and Sydney Uni — lived there most of my life but these days I live in Mullumbimby, a small town on the idyllic north coast of New South Wales, near Byron Bay. An hour and a half from Brisbane and a light year from reality, according to local wags. This is where I will be marching from to get to the crossbench in Canberra. Mullum, as we call it, is home to potheads, anxi-vaxxers and trustifarians. Less a base for an aspiring politician perhaps than a depot for people who can't construct a viable life anywhere else in the country. At the monthly markets you can purchase a wonderful array of artisanal goods and local produce including what are known as Chem-Trail Crystals. A sculptural object, basically a blob of multi-coloured quartz, designed to remove chem trails from your life, the toxic substances some believe are emitted by aircraft and cause cancer among other nasties. In other words, at Mullum Markets you can buy something that doesn't work to get rid of something that doesn't exist. That is my town. I came to the music festival here one year and stayed. Remarried, became a step-dad. It's great. But not everyone in Australia sees Mullum that way.

To be fair, Mullum is a curious place and though it remains defiantly alternative and a proud Green political stronghold, we have a surprising number of churches, including Seventh Day Adventist and Jehovah's Witness. It probably has an Amway Circle in the industrial estate. We certainly have more than one drumming circle and an abundance of windmill dancers. Mullum in fact is the broadest church full of brilliant people including entrepreneurs and best-selling authors, amazing musicians, genius farmers and all sorts of people living interesting self-determined lives. Come to Mullum Music Festival and you'll see what I mean — the whole town becomes the venue for a celebration of music that is hard to match anywhere, a triumph of human scale. But, here's the thing few people mention, increasingly it is a place people are moving to — like much of regional Australia — so they can live the good suburban life that is no longer possible for many in our cities. Mullum and places like it have become an attractive option for people who want to recreate for their children the childhoods they enjoyed in Sydney or Melbourne. Don't tell anyone because our housing stock is so limited that property prices are already berserk.

Overcoming Obstacles — Basic Beliefs

Rationally, I thought my beliefs would get in the way of a political career because they were not shared by the political class. To demonstrate my point: I believe that the self, the basic concept of the individual, is an illusion. This is because, it seems to me, that as soon as we start talking about who we are, we speak only of other people and things. The way we describe ourselves as individuals is basically a list of other people and things. For example: our kids and the way they run to the table at breakfast. Or a poem we love by Dylan Thomas or Emily Dickinson. The steep rise you cycle over every Saturday morning with mates you've had since school. The curious animal that is the red panda. The legal rights of rivers. Our mums. Rugs from western Rajasthan. Pineapple cheesecake. The ability to fix lawnmowers. That's a person. Ergo: the self is not really a thing. Got it?

Well, it occurred to me that this philosophy would be a hard sell in question-time. 'Honourable members I rise to point out that the self is an illusion, inimical, damaging, to human happiness. Once upon a time it was necessary to help us break from the yoke of medieval serfdom and superstition, but now it is the basis of our enslavement, the primary mechanism of oppression in our condition of post-industrial consumer capitalism'. I would lose the House with this kind of talk. The likes of Tony Abbott or Cory Bernardi might combust. But then I got to thinking that this was a risk worth taking. Friends, we have been sold the idea that humans are fundamentally selfish for years. That idea has fired an entire political and economic system based on greed and consumption. The Politics of Greed is not just wrong and harmful to us and our earth, it is based on a fantasy — the illusion of the self. Given a chance, people love to hang out together, to do things as a group, whether it's a footy team, a choir or a family picnic. We have been sold a grim lie for the benefit of the few: The Wealthier People over The Not So Wealthy. Simple!

Being A Grateful Person

To round out this section of personal reflection I should mention I am a grateful person. Grateful just to be alive at this time in human history, in this country, for all its improvement areas. My life has been unmarked by war or natural disaster. There have been only occasional, minor problems in my life. Nothing that a swim couldn't fix, as I like to say. Or a beer with a friend. Or a Nina Simone record. How good was she? One of the great musicians of the twentieth century and a radical black woman full of righteous anger at the stupidity and injustice of a world she did not design. If you want to be transported have a listen to 'Plain Gold Ring' or 'I Want A Little Sugar In My Bowl'.

As a Near Dead White Male, I am also deeply grateful that Chicxalub has never made an appearance in my diary. Not once, not on a single day in my life has an enormous rock appeared from the deep immensity of space and smashed into our fragile planet, annihilating most of its life forms. Yes! I am deeply grateful for that. I am grateful for the brief gift of consciousness and the privilege of being healthy and able to live a good life. Yet I look around me and I see a country that does not exactly seem to be defined by gratitude. Grateful is not what I see on the escalators at the shopping mall. What I often see instead is an 'oh shit, is this my life?' look on people's faces. A kind of sullen emptiness. People sick of looking for parking spots at the local shops and getting a ticket when they didn't see the sign limiting unmetered parking to the hours of 4am-6am every other Thursday. People sick of looking for bargains and buying things they don't need, things that don't work, or that fall apart. People spending too long on the phone to a call centre waiting to complain then losing the determination to do so because dinner needs to be cooked, nappies need to be changed, or a BAS needs to be done because the government turned you into a tax collector long, long ago and somehow that was accepted by people as normal and OK without so much as a whimper. People looking for jobs that aren't there in order to earn a meagre wage that is challenging if not impossible to live on.

I get it. There are reasons not to be grateful. We are a wealthy country but so much of our time is wasted or misdirected. And that's just during the pleasurable bits. It doesn't take into account the stress of having parents with dementia, kids with autism spectrum disorder or bosses with unmanageable levels of sociopathy. I really do get it. The result is an edgy sort of meaninglessness amid so much astonishing beauty and wealth. This feeling seems prevalent at the mall and I wonder sometimes if people think colonisation was worthwhile. Why did Europeans come here? Indigenous people must shake their heads at the culture white people introduced to their part of the planet and the strange relationship to happiness displayed by so many Australians.

Finally, I must also confess to being a slightly undisciplined person. If I walk past a homeless person I think to myself: 'but for a few twists of fate, that could be me'. I wonder if the members of our political class ever have that thought. And then, having walked on down the street, my mind full of the busy week ahead, I think: 'that set up doesn't look too bad. A pillow. A blanket. An alcove. A book. No phone'. These are not the thoughts of an aspiring politician, a leader of our nation. Too loose. Or maybe we need to loosen up, so our politicians can be more like we actually are and less like they think the people would like them to be.

Who should represent us?

Ok, that's enough self-reflection.

It is clear we should have more people in parliament who are more like the ordinary person. Not Old Mate who rails angrily against immigrants or campaigns for the return of the superphosphate bounty. No, someone like you or someone like me. Incidentally, I've always said that so-called red-necks would be a lot less racist if good jobs were a whole lot easier to find and keep, especially in regional Australia.

We need people in parliament who believe our government should be organised around our ordinary, unspectacular lives. A country that educates its people properly as an end in itself because knowledge and the life of the mind is important. A country where art matters. Where we work not to make mega-bucks but to create a decent society that will only get better, more enlightened and civilised in the future.

But look at the mob who currently rule over us. Take a good look at the photographs of our elected representatives. Visit the parliamentary website. They don't look much like the People of Australia, do they? They look airbrushed. Shaved and coiffed into similarity and anonymity. All the edges sanded back to the brink of the insipid. They ooze a kind of bogus respectability. Ready to say 'good to be with you' and 'thank you for your question' to anyone prepared to pretend to listen. Too ready. They are media trained. Equipped with the factory settings of the modern machine politician. They are absolutely the last people that should be representing you and your interests, governing this country and determining its future. Most of them. Too old. Too male. Too straight. Doesn't Pat Dodson stand out?

Whereas as you and I, the undisciplined and occasionally debauched, are exactly what the country needs. We are the people who make this bloody country what it is. Our democracy needs people like us. Yes, if, like me, you are possibly unfit by the standards of our political class, you are just what Australia needs. It turns out that We The People are the ones who can Make Australia Slightly Better Than Average Again™.

PART SIX:
Seriously. Fixing Australia.

My campaign to run for the Senate, to Rebuild our Common Wealth and Make Australia Slightly Better Than Average Again™ evolved from doing a show called 'Alternative Prime Minister'. It took me all over Australia, to comedy festivals and pubs and clubs. Small but tasteful venues. When talking to people after the shows it was impossible not to notice the thirst for change and for a different way of doing politics. People everywhere wanted to talk policy. From climate change to border control. From tax policy to industry development. I tried to stop them and failed. In this section we take the ideas of this book more seriously. The first bit is a hypothetical, an imagined message from a fictional Prime Minster. The second part is a policy statement that sets out policies and actions we could support, fund and develop to Make Australia Slightly Better Than Average Again™.

A Message from The Prime Minister
Imagine if you woke up one day and heard this on the radio from our prime minister.

Hello everyone. I want to talk to you about the future of this country. It seems to me that Australia needs a clearer story, a vision, a strategy for its future. We need to tell this story together as the People of Australia . . . I think the story starts like this.

We are a small country in a large world. We are a social democracy defined by our commitment to prosperity, learning and equality. We live together here with common interests. We are not as different from each other or the rest of the world as some say.

We are a prosperous country, grateful for our good fortune. Australia needs an economy that serves its people. We need to invest public and private resources to create a sustainable prosperity, based on technology, new agriculture and renewable energy. We can move from the old industries to the new; but the market cannot do this by itself. We need to harness our inventiveness. That inventiveness that revolutionised wifi. That inventiveness that made the stump jump plough. We make medical discoveries all the time. We even build amazing handcrafted pianos. We can invest in our creativity, build communities around that creativity and prosper together.

We need to be a country where we all live well. Australia needs an active and bold sovereign wealth fund to help make that happen. Driven by superannuation savings, we can invest in the industries of our future — in renewables, technology and agriculture to create wealth; in housing, health and the arts to build liveable communities. This fund will be at the centre of our government and national conversations.

We will reward citizens who invest in our nation and its communities and not artificial structures that minimise tax. We will tax people to encourage prosperity. Too much money is tied up in tricks and trusts when it could be spent employing people and building communities and businesses. We need incentives to invest and employ because too much money and opportunity is leaving the country.

Australia is a land of small businesses and we need to build communities around their prosperity. We will work together to build your business. Community-owned banks and health funds, energy generators, call centres and medical centres can grow. Success must not be measured by reducing tax.

Australia must be a country that learns and keeps learning. We can invest in our citizens and offer free first degrees; we can export our education to the world. We need to get the balance in our universities right, with the humanities and pure sciences as important as vocational and commercial degrees. Learning is an endless end in itself.

Australia should be a constructive global citizen; we will foster prosperity and democracy in the Pacific and Asia; we will break from our colonial past and work with our neighbours as partners; we will speak up on human rights consistently and get our own house in order.

Australia will be a practical force for peace in the world. We will not participate in wars that are not in our interest; nor will we buy armaments we do not need. Given the choice we will invest in development in other countries and not war. We will not encourage fear or talk up terrorism. We will be measured in our response to threats and spend our dollars wisely.

Australia will better look after its own; we will rehabilitate offenders and minimise incarceration; victims will be heard and compensated; we will resource our police and courts to deliver justice; we will reconnect offenders with their communities; the worst offenders will not define our system.

Australia will encourage diversity and creativity. Our many different peoples must be able to pursue their identities and build their communities as they wish, with freedom, respect and support. Everyone must be able to live according to what they believe; and we will share a peaceful public life where we come together to be more than the sum of our parts.

Australia is a beautiful country but it has been abused. We need to repair and nurture the land — from our rivers to the reef. A balance needs to be found that allows us a good standard of living within a recovering world. If we need to consume less, to have less, then so be it. Nature can power our future. Renewables are really the future of our workers.

Australia is an ancient land and its future begins with its past, with the people who were first here and are still here. We need to sit down and make treaties, create an advisory council to government and a national reconciliation fund. We need to achieve reconciliation, together, we need to make deep amends, to tell the truth of our past and begin again.

We need to be an Australia that builds and cherishes its Common Wealth.

How would you feel if you heard that kind of talk? Some of you might think ok, well what next? As the Prime Minister asks in this letter, where would you take the story from here?

Write your thoughts, comments and feelings here. Neatly. Or not.

So seriously what would you do?

Every now and then over a beer or coffee or dinner with old friends, the question is asked: 'so, seriously, what would you do if you ran the country and had a blank slate?' In this section, I try to answer that question, with a clear statement of what we might do, given half a chance. What follows is a series of policies expressed in simple terms at light speed. A bit of a Soundbite Manifesto, if you like, for a Government that is dedicated to Rebuilding our Common Wealth.

Some of us balk at the idea of ordinary people proposing government policy. We think we lack expertise or experience. Even if we do, I would like to challenge this status quo on policy making and the public debate of political issues. Our policy development has been constipated for some time. We need to loosen our minds to make progress. For example, in housing policy our politicians can't seem to get past a miserably narrow debate about negative gearing as if tweaking a single tax break can address the myriad problems of supply and affordability. Where is the experience and expertise in that?

We all know the saying that politics is the art of the possible. To keep our ambitions to minimum, I guess. Then again I would not have thought it possible for our politics to have become what it now is during my lifetime. Our very idea of the possible has become impoverished. And that is no good at all for anyone, whatever your politics, whatever your life is about.

My list is not complete but it shows how easily the conversation can move from business tax cuts or more for Medicare to a broader plan for a future for Australia. It is incredibly ambitious but the primary idea here is to try to bring all of the big issues together and consider them all at once. Our politics is currently very single issue oriented. If you find yourself thinking 'wow, how would you fund that?', maybe you could try to answer that question. The first section below is entitled

Better Spending — much of it is about how we can redirect money we currently spend in government, so there is no new funding required.

However, some new taxes will be needed. We should not be afraid of that. Taxation, in fact, is the main way of redistributing wealth to achieve a fairer society. That is how taxation has been used for a long time. Put another way, taxation is about funding Australia's shared, public, goods or services that we all benefit from, rather than private goods or services whose benefits are narrower. Taxation seems to carry an automatically negative connotation these days and that is a shame because taxation is — if you stop to think about it — an investment in the Common Wealth of Australia, in so many of the things that we use and enjoy, and that, to be fair, already do Make Australia Slightly Better Than Average™.

My Three Key Themes are:

1. Better Spending
2. Better Society
3. Better Government.

My whole platform is a case for the return and restoration of Government in the public interest, from public broadcasting to a national ICAC, from stopping privatisation to tenure for public servants, from boosting legal aid to going long on scientific research. Government as an active, constructive force for positive change. How does that sound?

And don't forget, in The Real World, governments are generally elected on a lot less policy detail than this. The other big policy they are elected on is this one: change as little as possible. You will not find that policy anywhere in my Soundbite Manifesto.

Better spending

We can make a huge difference in government over time by spending money differently, changing our priorities and spending existing revenues better:

- We should invest in learning not defence. We could move half the defence budget into education and research. That's around $15 billion per year. It would allow us to subsidise free undergraduate university education, rebuild TAFE and fund scientific research. Australia is not capable of independent defence and remains valuable to strategic partners. The recent growth in the defence budget should be turned back and redirected into education to support our future economic and social development.
- We can be a renewables superpower by moving fossil fuel subsidies and exploration incentives across to renewables such as solar and wind. That's estimated to be over $10 million a year, which will provide a platform to attract investment in a key new industry. Historically, energy has been a state-run business, and the privatisation of the sector has only resulted in dysfunction, unemployment and higher retail prices. Government investment in industry development is inevitable and should favour the future: renewables.
- The existing bank tax yielding $1–2 billion per annum can be earmarked for small business development, especially in regional Australia, funding incentives to employ and train workers including apprentices, with a dedicated development fund for mutual and co-operative businesses that put their communities before profits.
- We spend billions on border control and detention centres in the Pacific and those funds could be better spent improving on-shore criminal justice in rehabilitation, victim compensation and

community integration programs, along with investing in regional development to support refugees and asylum seekers.

We can also refresh the way we fund government services or projects and raise tax:

- A turbo-charged sovereign wealth fund — with a board appointed by the federal parliament — should tap superannuation funds and redirect offshore investment into key infrastructure projects. The fund could support partial re-nationalisation or government statutory corporations in key industries such as electricity, transport and banking.
- A new land tax paid by all land owners — working with the states and replacing stamp duty — would add billions to revenue and fund an affordable public housing scheme, addressing the existing market failure for lower and middle income housing. Reducing the discount for capital gains taxes could also boost revenue.
- Universal basic income — government income support can start with a basic safety net for all citizens, with top ups for disability, aged pension, veterans and unemployment. Basic income for people without work (e.g. Newstart) should be significantly increased. The system should be based on providing subsistence rather than economic utility.
- High income earners should contribute to the federal budget through a Buffett-style tax. People earning say $250,000 or more would pay an agreed percentage of their income — a flag fall — in tax each year. The minimum rate paid should be no less than the GST.
- Corporate turnover tax — this would ensure companies contribute to government revenues, even when their income tax would otherwise be zero. A corporate equivalent to the Buffett tax. Related tax reforms could include a stock exchange transaction tax.

- Public Health — Medicare Levy and health insurance rebates should be reviewed; reducing public funding of private health cover and boosting public health spending.
- Public Schools — public education needs to be rebooted and renewed. Private school funding should be reviewed and reduced with a boost to public school spending.
- Indigenous justice — a treaty levy could fund the compensation, development and reconciliation projects that flow from treaties negotiated with indigenous Australia.
- Public broadcasting guarantee — funding for the ABC and SBS can be doubled in year one followed by a fixed, statutory 10 per cent increase for 10 years.
- Federalism — we need to review the fundamentals of federalism and articulate clear principles for government and revenue sharing. The level and use of GST should match government priorities.
- Key worker investment — we need to invest in valued key workers like nurses, teachers, police and firies across the country.
- Middle class welfare — phasing out superannuation exemptions and introducing means tests for all tax benefits can lower government spending and release funds for other programs.
- Religious institutions tax — larger religions that hold land and generate income should pay land and turnover taxes at a rate between charities and businesses (say 10% of income, the rate of the GST).
- Development Tax — a Robin Hood tax applied to cross-border financial transactions could fund regional development and an international aid budget up to 0.7 per cent of GDP.
- Budget Strategy — a Federal Spending Ombudsman should be created to set surplus and deficit targets and to manage a long-term bi-partisan budget strategy.

- Climate Change Fund — positioned as a long-term investment in our future and significant job creator across the country.

Better Society

We need to be more active in shaping our society, making bigger and better policy decisions to create the Australia we want. Government can take action to bring our future to life:

- Indigenous Australia should be able to negotiate treaties with the federal and state governments, supported by advisory councils in all Australian parliaments and a national indigenous compensation and development fund, financed by a federal Treaty levy.
- National Industry Policy must be central to government — we need a clear set of priorities, targets and funding commitments for developing our current and future technology, agriculture and energy businesses. We need a story of economic development over the longer-term and genuine policies that help Australia get there.
- A turbo-charged sovereign wealth fund can lead the implementation of national industry policy with a key strategic and funding role for government as investor and partner. Incentives are required to keep investment in Australia to support infrastructure development rather than chasing profits overseas.
- A housing strategy and fund should be a key government activity with federal and state governments returning to active community development, working in partnership with councils, communities and developers to deliver better public and private housing. Superannuation funds should receive incentives to invest in lower and middle income housing.

- The minimum wage should be boosted so that companies and government share the cost of subsistence and minimum livelihood standards for our workers.
- The NBN should be wholly owned and operated in perpetuity by a statutory corporation, supported by all political parties. Our technology platform is too important, too fundamental, to our society and economic development to be politicised.
- Our national energy policy must manage the transition to renewables with a rational phase-out strategy for coal; with emissions targets benchmarked to the best international standards and with the goal of moving towards 100% renewables in the medium term.
- Free undergraduate university and TAFE education should be reintroduced for all Australians, offering a three-year course at no cost to citizens and permanent residents. Over time, the commercialisation of universities should be moderated.
- Legal aid for lower income Australians needs to be improved covering all crime, domestic violence, family law, immigration and some personal injury. Legal Aid and community legal centres must be expanded to deliver the required services.
- Women need to be more prominent in government policy with violence within families and reproductive rights given more focus and funding. We need to listen to women.
- Unions must be strengthened with clearer rights to strike and organise. The right to strike is a human right; workers control little beyond their capacity to withdraw labour.
- We need a serious arts policy and funding to ensure the arts thrive in our communities. Existing arts budgets are paltry and constant cuts undermine the crucial creative and economic contributions made by the arts to our communities.

- Public broadcasting is an important social objective of Australian life, equal to public health, education and transport.
- Business and Society — Law reform can replace profit maximisation with more balanced obligations for companies and businesses. Financial planners and estate agents should be paid hourly rates not commission fees and have fiduciary duties to their clients.
- NGOs can be supported by an expanded DGR (Deductible Gift Recipient) scheme encouraging donations — voluntary tax — that contribute to building our Common Wealth.

Better Government

We need a more responsive and democratic government engaged with the people. We need to restore and grow better institutions that serve the public interest:

- Government should report annually to Australian Citizens on the return on investment for money spent in every project, fund and department, as a company reports to its shareholders.
- Privatisation as government policy should be suspended pending a royal commission into the impact of privatisation on Australian society and its economy. A new model for running statutory corporations in key industries (banking, energy, transport, telecommunications) will be developed.
- Government tender processes should be completely transparent with commercial confidentiality ending once the tender is awarded.
- Administration of taxpayer funded services should remain under government control. For example the Land Titles Office and social security payment collection ought to be managed by the state.

- Justice should be the responsibility of the state. Private prisons can provide incentives to incarcerate. Private contractors should be phased out.

- Detention centres will be closed down. In Australia or offshore, the government should not jail people who have not committed crimes and never for indefinite periods.

- Significant strategic decisions need a super-majority of both houses of parliament. Such decisions might include referendum proposals, decisions to go to war or material changes to the treaty or international status of Australia (e.g. ANZUS, ASEAN, TPP).

- Election campaigns should be publicly funded with capped private donations from individuals and companies permitted.

- Lobbyists should be publicly listed on a register with access to politicians and their remuneration sources disclosed. Private access to ministers should be banned.

- Public service tenure must be restored, with staff contracts extended to encourage independence. Expenditure on outsourcing should be reduced to fund the initiative.

- Consultant fees — we need real-time public disclosure of the fees paid to consultants by government to do work once done by public servants.

- A bill of rights binding on all governments that enacts basic rights consistent with United Nations standards including social, civil and political rights, criminal procedure rights and environmental and economic rights.

- Failing NGO service providers should be re-nationalised; for example in employment services, vocational education and disability services.

- Regulation should be boosted by providing additional resources to ASIC, the ACCC and APRA. Better staff with genuine career paths are needed to make regulation work.

- An accountability and corruption watchdog modelled on the state-based corruption bodies is required to properly monitor performance in government.
- Water is a key national resource that needs to be federally managed in a transparent market. An independent authority should manage national water allocation and use.
- Climate change projects remediating and preparing for further impacts on our coastlines, rivers and forests need to be developed and properly funded. Initiatives should be connected to the Sovereign Wealth Fund and National Industry Policy. The health of the Great Barrier Reef should be the barometer of our success in living within and restoring our environment.
- Self-determination: Australia should be a republic with a president as its elected head of state chosen by a majority of adult voters.

Your Turn

What do you think of that list? Does it make you think? Does it make you wonder what might be possible? What would you like to add? What would you change?

This list could not possibly be exhaustive. These dot points are mere soundbites but the overall impression is what counts. We too often think of one issue in isolation rather than the totality of government. And we need to do more of that. We need to think long term and have complex debates about the choices we make as a country through the various priorities of and investments made by government.

I will use these ideas in my campaign — for speeches and videos, blog posts and posters. And if I get elected to the Senate, my decisions will be based on this way of thinking. But I want to know what you think. Because this is just an outline, a start of a long-term project.

So . . . what are your ideas for Better Spending. Better Society. Better Government? You might need a bigger box. Maybe a whiteboard. Go for it!

PART SEVEN:
A few personal observations

Welcome to Part Seven. This section is a kind of essay about the current political moment in Australia as we approach yet another federal election and how we — and I — got here. It's humorous but sincere, and includes a few digressions into my own mis-adventures in politics and finishes with a rousing metaphor (including Hula Hoops) that everyone is encouraged to try out at home.

Airport Security

You could be forgiven for thinking the only growth sector in The Economy is airport security. I think it's good that so many people thrown out of crap jobs in factories and warehouses, shopping malls and call centres, get work at our airports. I hope they can now afford to make homes and raise families if they want that. At the same time, we have no money for artists and can't pay our nurses properly. But if you have a talent for frisking people, it's come on down and report for duty. Airport Security is huge! Honestly, how many people does it take to work out whether you've left your scissors in your carry-on? The airport staff rooms must be massive. I worry about where they fit everyone. How big is the locker area for the airport security team?

If you're like me you probably get asked to do the explosives test when you go through the security checkpoint and your flight is boarding and it's down to the final call. Guaranteed. When the departure board starts flashing, a person in uniform approaches you, someone you know is struggling to keep their life together because no one would choose to do the explosives test job. It is not a dream job. It is not a career to be passionate about. It is the kind of job you might lie to your spouse about. 'Ah I work with fertilisers, love' you might say at family events like the evening meal. You certainly wouldn't mention it on Tinder.

The uniformed fellow citizen always chooses me and asks: 'would you mind doing an explosives test?' I want to say 'would you like me to explode?' I want to step back and wait for the reaction from the Easter Island face of Australian authority. Hoping for a smirk. But I don't — and nor do you — because humour is banned at our airports. Yes, in this country of the larrikin it is a crime to crack a funny. I would love to change that somehow. Humour should be mandatory at Airport Security, if only to make the job of the uniformed operative a little more bearable. Can you imagine looking for nail scissors and lighters all day? If you think I'm being flippant here, I ask you, 'Would checking for nail scissors have stopped 9/11?'

Airport security makes me sad because it shows that we are prepared to invest massively in the industry of fear while other parts of our society are neglected. I do not have graphs to make my point but it would be interesting to see the relative trajectories of arts funding in Australia over the last 20 years and the investment in airport security. Makes me weep.

The Limits of Satire

Because we have banned this site-specific genre of humour we head home for a dose of professional political satire. The deal is that you get to laugh at the foibles of our leaders and system then do nothing about it. As a consumer of political satire, you get a slightly sickening feeling of being smarter, even better, than the people engaged in government, and that's the end of the section.

Consider the ABC's *Utopia*, a program that reliably skewers its targets. Failed infrastructure projects. Hopeless ministers. Blatant pork-barrelling. You might find yourself as I do sitting on your Nick Scali leather three-piece enjoying an episode that proves beyond reasonable doubt the intractable, inescapable horror of our fecklessness in government administration. You slurp your way through a bottle of reasonably priced, reasonably good Pinot Noir. You might mumble to your snoozing life partner: 'it's uncanny, my love, it's just like my work, dead set, there's no strategy, no follow-through, no cut-through, no vision, no . . . nothing'. Then you nod off, delighted that the ABC can still make a good show, before waking in fright around 3am, to a red wine-infused dribble cascading its way down between the leather cushions of the lounge suite onto the new Tuscan tiles.

Or is that just me? The trouble is, you know the facts about the subject being satirised because you are a dedicated professional with a nuanced appreciation of the challenges of contemporary government. And sometimes the Pinot Noir doesn't work. Sometimes, as you blink in the dark of your home theatre at 3.15am, you have to admit to yourself that:

- Interest rates have never been lower but the economy is barely growing.
- Taxes and government debt are also low but the politicians insist they are not.

- Public servants cannot get decisions made and are terrified of losing their jobs.
- Jobless numbers are good but you know heaps of kids and oldies who can't get a job.
- One in six kids lives below the poverty line — over 15% of our children. What the ... ?
- Thousands of armed service veterans are homeless. Thank you for your service!
- The government talks up terrorism while talking down climate change. How?

You find yourself still awake at 4.42am watching the replay of the under 21s water polo between Australia and Hungary from the world champs in Caracas on the 45-inch screen. Then you think a thought almost impossible to express, even to your life partner or counsellor. 'Political satire hasn't really changed anything about the way we live. I loved Max Gillies back in the '80s. Denton, The D-Generation. The Chaser. They've changed nothing. None of them. Even John Clarke.' The world has gotten appreciably worse. I know the stats. It's much madder. I'm sure it's not just me.

We Need An Alternative Prime Minister

Do we what!

You often hear the Opposition Leader described as the Alternative Prime Minister. But we could really use a genuinely alternative prime minister. One that reflects the country and who can tell the story of our future. One that is not a Near Dead White Male for starters. So that rules me out from the very beginning. We have had enough of them, haven't we?

I would love to see a genuine alternative PM like a young indigenous woman from the Kimberleys or Arnhem Land, with a deadly burlesque routine and a background in civil engineering. A professional person, with a creative side. A thinker and a mover. A young woman who would offer a different view of the country. I would love to see what someone like that could do to change Australia. Mind you, I would not want to ruin her life by exposing her to machine politics in Canberra.

I also have moments when I think Penny Wong would make a good prime minister; there is a steel in her that appeals to me and she embodies in many good ways our changing Australia. Mind you, as a senior Labor figure who has supported the main policies of our political class, Penny cannot be excused from the crimes of our oppressors. But, she is plainly made of the right stuff. Tonka tough. Penny has succeeded in our toxic political system despite being Asian, lesbian . . . and from Adelaide. What a champion. For all that, I would not wish the role upon Penny either. I just like her too much and have only warm feelings for her family. I would not wish the top job even on Andrew Bolt. Then again . . .

I reckon we have a real crisis of talent in our politics. We have amazing people in all walks of life. We have world beaters in global business and the arts, in sports and science. We win Oscars, Fields Medals, World Cups. Australia, as it should given our wealth, our weather and our education system, produces extraordinary people. A few make it into parliament but not as many as we would like. The idea that only the best among us get into leadership roles in our parties has long been seen as ridiculous. For so many people who could make a contribution, the calculus is this: are you prepared to give up the interesting and rewarding things you might do with your life to participate in a broken system? And before that, before you get into parliament, are you able to endure the internal shenanigans and skullduggery of a political party?

The Other Bloke: You Know . . . er . . . him.

As we go to print, the incumbent Alternative Prime Minister is, as usual, the leader of the opposition. What's his name? You know . . . That bloke. With the big head who lost a lot of weight in a hurry and looks lost in a suit. He's from Melbourne, I think. Worked for a union for a while. Never had a real job. Never been a merchant banker or even a lawyer.

Um Bill Shorten. That's it. Had to Google him. Another Near Dead White Male. There is something spectacularly unspectacular about Bill. His party has enjoyed a lead in the polls since the last election (2016), even though most of the electorate doesn't know who he is. That is quite a feat when his basic job is to be known by the voters of the country. Amazing, in fact. Particularly given that government ministers cannot get through a single interview without talking about Bill and blaming him for every ill in the country from national security to the shrinking of Iced Vo-Vo biscuits. Usually in the first sentence.

The Alternative PM is not well liked by the People of Australia. Some say Bill is a social-climbing suck-hole. But that's unfair. The available evidence suggests it was a complete fluke that Bill's second wife turned out to be the daughter of the Governor General. That happens with all Labor leaders. To be clear, I make no judgment on the number of Bill's marriages — for the record I can beat him at that game. But it remains odd that Shorten says 'wiff' instead of 'with'. It would be unkind to mention this had Bill not been educated at a posh private school and university. There must be something wrong wiff the man.

The problem with Bill is he has such a hard-on for the Lodge. We The People don't like that. He is the ultimate machine politician. Despite an obvious lack of charisma, Shorten has risen to lead a cutthroat political operation that literally devours and destroys the weak. Bill has turned knifing leaders — Rudd for Gillard and then Gillard for Rudd — into an art form that would impress a rogue sashimi chef. Bill has been a future

PM since he was seven and nothing else. As a union organiser straight out of Monash University, Bill was already jockeying for the Lodge. He locked onto the mission like a goanna to a German bushwalker's leg. His execution of two prime ministers were mere sub-plots to Shorten's big dream to be the School Captain of Australia.

Now here's a story I can't corroborate but what the hey. One Christmas at Myers in Melbourne Bill sat on Santa's knee and was asked, 'So what do you want in your stocking this year, little man?' Whereupon Bill replied: 'Thank you for your question, Leigh. Good to be with you. I know what I want for Christmas because I know what I want to do wiff my life . . . (Pause) . . . Let me answer (Pause) . . . I want to be prime minister'. Santa took a swig from his brandy and fired back: 'Geez, you're only 7 little fella, keep a lid on that sorta talk. And my name is Bob, not Leigh'. Little Bill chipped: 'Yeah, isn't it great that I know what I want to do wiff my brief time on earth, Laurie?' Santa then gave young Shorten a clip around the ear. Sadly the floor manager saw the incident and Bob lost his job. Santa's full name was Bob Santamaria, not the famous one who started The Movement but a green grocer in Smith Street, Collingwood who went broke after a supermarket chain opened in 1971, ruining Bob, the Hungarian deli across the road and a frozen goods business a bloke originally opened with the proceeds of a single nugget mined outside Ballarat in 1859. Anyway, old Bob told little Bill what he thought: 'we prefer our PMs to be self-effacing like John Curtin or convinced of their magnificence like Whitlam or Menzies. You haven't got it, pal. Take up something safe, like a record store. There's a gap in that market. Edels and Palings don't look after the customers. Mark my words!'

Of course Bill didn't take Santa's advice, and at the time of writing is poised to become the Stephen Bradbury of Australian politics — the last man standing on our thin political ice. Remember the skater who won Olympic gold when all the other competitors fell over? Yes. Bill

Shorten. Our next PM. Well, anything is possible in this wonderful but addled country, isn't it? Let me apologise for implanting the image of Bill in lycra in your minds. It will stay with you all week. Funny to think this, but I can't imagine Bill doing the wild thing. Can you? I struggle to see him doing anything not directly associated with his Grand Journey to the Lodge. Can Bill ride a bike? Can you see him windsurfing? I could always imagine Mal and Lucy getting into it, in the mansion at Point Piper. In the library, with the Labrador looking on, dribbling on the Russell Drysdale place-mats he got as a gift from Tim Fischer. I can see all that. But not Bill.

So, we doubt Shorten because his work has been all politics and ambition and he lacks a certain life experience. He's different from Paul Keating, the David Campese of the ALP or Bob Hawke, the Jack Thompson — who had their own unique charisma. Despite all this I could just about accept Shorten as prime minister. Like you might take a schooner of VB at a country pub around 10pm on a Monday night because there's no other beer left. Because, on balance, the ALP is a slightly better version of the bad song that is #auspol and has had its moments in our history. Some of them great. But Shorten really does promise to deliver the dullest government in our history. Slightly fairer taxes. Tinkering with negative gearing. A little more renewable energy. A few bob for schools and hospitals. A ham-and-pineapple pizza of a government, washed down with mid-strength beer. An average government. Frankly, Shorten's calculated gutlessness over national security, refugees and human rights makes my blood boil. His parroting of the politics of Opportunity over Outcome also makes me wonder fundamentally about whose side he is on. We The People deserve better than Bill.

Remembering Malcolm Turnbull

Briefly. I used to think of Malcolm Turnbull as the Wretched Incumbent. I had a theory that he was only PM because he couldn't face the idea of being retired: taking the grandkids for food court lunches, losing tennis to his father-in-law, Tom Hughes, and reading Proust again in his dressing gown. Turnbull's legacy is sad, and laughable really, seeing he was his generation's natural prime minister. But what he should be remembered for is being our first fully self-funded PM. We seem to forget that he spent $1.75m of his own coin on campaign advertising — when his government won by a single seat in 2016. If he hadn't stumped up they may well have lost. It's odd that Turnbull sustained no political damage for this blatant self-investment. Where was the Tall Poppy Syndrome when we needed it, huh?

In the beginning, when Turnbull unseated the Uber-bloke Beta-male Tony Abbott, some brave souls likened Our Mal to Gough Whitlam, an intellectual leader who would recreate the nation in his own image. Yeah, right. Then again, Australia had already been (partially) recreated in his image as a country of selfish, aspirational materialists out of touch with the best of our traditions and with no idea of our future. Turnbull, as we now know, believed in nothing, not even his own supposed ideas — whether the Republic or renewable energy or even the rule of law. He believed only in his position, making him the epitome of his mob — a whole class of people who have done little but settle into the bureaucracy of Australian capitalism, enjoying their pockets of privilege, as the country slowly unravelled into the post-democratic, post-meaning, fractious blur of anxious vagueness that #auspol is today. In the end, having removed two leaders on his scramble to the top, he finally got the arse for good, for reasons that remain obscure. Hoo roo!

The Second Most Important Person in Australia

I am a cricket tragic and proud of it. I first went to the SCG to see a test match with my dad in 1974 aged 7. So I grew up with the now quaint idea that the second most important person in Australia is the Captain of the Australian Cricket Team, behind the Prime Minister, of course. Maybe this crazy notion helps explain the astonishing response to Sandpapergate: a scandal that saw Steve Smith, the then-captain of our team with his deputy, Dave Warner, and a junior player, Cam Bancroft, create a moment of national disgrace. No one died. There was no robbery. It was far, far worse than that. In early 2018 Australia came to a standstill when our top cricketers cheated in South Africa. In plain sight. On global TV.

The Aussies and Saffers are great rivals. Similar countries. Hard-bitten competitive people with difficult histories, to wrap our shared colonial past in euphemism. The tide was turning against Australia. We were losing our grip on the game and the series. And so the ball was sanded. To gain an advantage by getting the thing to swing. Reverse swing. Sandpaper. On the field. This is not normal. This is not in the rules. And they got caught. Big mistake.

First, why would anyone take sandpaper on to a cricket field? Leave it in the shed, fellas. The lads were on tour, though. South Africa is different from Australia, a challenging environment for suburban boys raised on PlayStation and Domino's Pizza. Maybe they were homesick for the simple Australian pleasures like sanding a dining table for the family. Second, they got caught. What a bunch of dickheads! That's the first rule of cheating, isn't it? Do not get caught. And that's hard with 127 cameras trained on the ground.

For 72 hours Austraya was in moral uproar. As a tragic, this was hard for me to credit. Even people who didn't watch or play cricket had an opinion about the drama because our national honour was at stake.

Was it, really, I thought? It was amazing how strong the response was, the sheer depth of feeling as if a game of sport or a team — even the Australian Cricket Team — could possibly be that important to anyone. Never mind the indefinite detention of asylum seekers or women dying from domestic violence, our top cricketers were caught cheating! And they admitted it. Eventually (after a laughable effort at a cover-up).

It set me thinking as I was planning this book on how you cannot pick what will wind up the Australian people. For my entire adult life we have been chipping away at government — once the binding force of Australian communities. And few of us seem fussed. Sure government can get out of hand and needs to be handled well, like a dog. But also like a dog, government can be the best of us. It can embody our egalitarian myth and make it live. Unfortunately, the damage done is starting to show. The state of the NBN alone should have us on the streets. Why do we not care about that like we cared about Sandpapergate? Why are we bought off so easily with tax cuts . . . with dog biscuits? To continue the analogy, it is like we are saying to our dogs, hey here's an extra biscuit — no, go on take two — but um, here's the thing, you'll have to build your own kennel now and find your own blanket. Because that's what Tax Cuts are — dog biscuits to suck on as the kennel burns.

Perhaps we reacted so strongly because we know the realities of life and government are hard to shift. The madness of our political life might make us believe in silly things, like the spirit of fair play in cricket, even more ardently, more desperately. Do we somehow project our need to believe in something onto a group of men who — being professionals of the modern era — have literally done nothing as adults except play cricket and turn up at events for their sponsors? Of course, the connection I would make here, given the themes of this book, is that there was a failure of leadership in this moment. It wasn't caused by the momentary weakness of the skipper or his deputy or the young player who did the deed. But a systemic failure. A culture that says winning is everything. Just as our banking sector and business generally puts profits before people. The evidence is mounting everywhere — from banks charging dead people to corner stores and fancy restaurants blithely underpaying workers.

In the wash-up of Sandpapergate it is remarkable that no one at Cricket Australia in the top executive ranks or on the board took the rap. Instead, they left the players concerned to suffer the consequences. Mark my words, Australian cricket sustained a life-threatening blow that day and it showed all of us what so-called leadership in this country has become. That is why, deep down, the reaction was so visceral and slightly unhinged. It wasn't about cheating. It was about the unwelcome truths about who our leaders are and what we allow them to be, about what Australia has become.

A confession — Granddad, Gough and dabbling in politics

Here is a real dog's leg and you might like to skip this bit, or not. You might have similar stories. I often hear people talking about their own difficult dabblings in politics. Many of us have a go and walk away disheartened. So, my confession is this: I have had a come-and-go relationship with politics throughout my life. I love politics and loathe party politics. All at once. Here are the highlights of my risible efforts, starting back in the 1970s in suburban Sydney.

I first learnt of politics when I was a kid watching television with my grandfather. A stern but loving man, Granddad kissed his wife every day as he left for work. A book-keeper and former soldier who lost an eye playing darts in the barracks at Bundock St, Randwick during the Second World War. He kept a jar of garlic gloves soaked in vinegar in the fridge through winter to ward off colds. Patrick Francis Kelly, known to everyone as Frank, loved his B&H special filter cigarettes but loathed communism, like many poor, working class Catholic Irish Australians did in those days.

When Gough Whitlam was elected my Granddad nearly had a stroke. We watched the 1972 election together on black and white television. I was 6. He was 68. We watched on Channel 10, because he loved *MASH* and Benny Hill. We even watched *Number 96*! Channel 10 was his station rather than the ABC which mum and dad watched downstairs in the rumpus room. I liked Channel 10 because they used the Richard Harris version of *Macarthur Park* as the theme music. Old Frank only lasted another few years before he carked it getting out of a cab on Maroubra Road, returning from doing the accounts for a chocolate maker in Toongabbie — a four-hour daily commute. A massive coronary. Granddad was a legend to me but spent his last few years hating Gough and voting for the Democratic Labor Party — rebels from the ALP who were economic nationalists but socially conservative in a way that is hard to imagine now. It's weird. Granddad never owned a house or a car but was terrified that the Communists could come and take from him everything he owned. Namely, a few LPs from the World Record Club, a shed full of carpenter's tools, some nice Vok glassware, a homemade spirit level and the Pears' Encyclopaedia for the crossword.

Granddad's loathing became my love. The way Gough spoke, his confidence, his cadence impressed me even though at six I had a dim idea of what he was about. You could feel the excitement in the community though. Even mum and dad were excited. They had badges saying It's Time. We had a poster in the study with Gough on it. Over the years, my love for Gough deepened, along with his vision of an Australia that was smart and caring, that was brave enough to want to change things for the better, an Australia that scared the hell out of a lot of people who felt they had something to lose. Gough became something like my ultimate football team. I would follow Club Gough for life, like many of my friends.

Obviously, to many conservatives, Gough is like Collingwood or Manly — the team everyone loves to hate. Dad once voted for Menzies but was generally a Labor supporter as was mum. Both my parents grew up in Coogee with the one pair of shoes which they only wore when forced to like most people growing up in small rented flats in Sydney during the Second World War. Dad became a high school teacher and mum was a 'front-office lady' who could've run the Department of Education in a different time. From 1972, they both voted for Labor at every election — council, state and federal.

Gough Whitlam still enrages conservatives. He was seen as a reckless spender, a big government guy. But the record suggests he established the modern agenda of Australia based on public health and education, industry development, law reform, independent foreign policy and progressive social policy. Overturning his legacy remains a key theme of right-wing politics today — if you need evidence browse through the publications of the Institute of Public Affairs (or mark his own party's abandonment of his platform). But Gough was no infallible god. He sold out Timor to the Indonesians and couldn't control an unruly and inexperienced ministry. He also chose some sketchy ministers. But his vision of a country striving to educate itself, to become a fairer society, to have better schools and health and infrastructure, to be part of the larger, complex world remains a damn good vision.

Gough was the first prime minister I remember and he inspired lots of school kids around me. At South Coogee Primary a girl called Cathy was tipped by everyone to one day get the top job. Cathy seemed almost cursed to be PM. Most schools had someone who stood out like her. We were doing finger-painting or learning to count with Cuisenaire rods while Cathy was planning her path to The Lodge. She had an uncanny self-belief and well combed hair. Cathy was fearless when doing class presentations and talked easily to adults.

People talked up Cathy at South Coogee and she liked it. Loved it, in truth! Cathy would tell people how much she wanted to be prime minister one day. Hit by the Bill Shorten stick. Most of us would have been happy playing footy for the Rabbitohs or sitting on Johnny Young's knee like Tiny Tina Arena. Here's the thing: after I left South Coogee Primary I did not hear of Cathy again. I have a vision of her running a regional government department in Coffs Harbour, with a great house on the water at Woolgoolga. A convertible, a cat and Jazz Ballet on Thursday nights. But not PM.

The memory of Cathy haunts me a little and reminds me of my own childhood pain. Yes, People of Australia, I briefly had delusions about politics as a kid. To explain . . . I was shy and skinny early on and got bullied. My nemesis was a bloke a few years above me called Gisli Bergman who opened the bowling for our second eleven. One day after school he and his henchmen grabbed me in the school gym and beat me up. I still don't know why. Perhaps he didn't like Gough either? Gisli didn't seem like a DLP supporter, though. It shook me up and to get me out of myself my parents encouraged me to take up debating. I did well. A bit of a monster was born — a public speaker — and I got bullied some more.

All this debating and speaking, much of it inspired by Gough, led me to the Labor Party. I went to my first meeting as a teenager when Bob Carr (future Premier and Foreign Minister) was our local member. I shook Bob's hand, expecting to be immediately recognised as a future PM. Like Cathy Worthington. Or at least education minister. But Bob looked at me in my crystal cylinders top and grey Californians like the skinny kid I was, a kid who should be at home watching the AMCO Cup. I thought I had found my patron. But, no. Turned out that listening to old people from the local chemical plant argue about uranium mining and the national wage case wasn't always as interesting as watching Easts v Wests from Leichhardt Oval with my mates and I soon drifted away.

A few years later at Sydney Uni I got involved in Young Labor which basically operated as a refuge for youngsters who couldn't find a 'cuddle' anywhere else. To be honest, it was a blur of wanking and Clearasil. But seriously, I had a red hot go. One day we were at state conference lining up the votes behind a bloke called Anthony Albanese — a good man — to take up positions in the secretariat, in order to secure a critical advantage for the left faction of the party. One of the organisers of our group asks us for volunteers. Someone was to ring up the leader of the hated right faction on the morning of the big vote to divert them from the conference venue. This directive was given with solemnity, as if the fate of western democracy turned on it. I was shocked. I make no claim that Young Albo endorsed it, but the plan was to call this poor bloke and tell him his sister had been in a massive car accident, was in emergency at Royal Prince Alfred Hospital and hadn't he better go see if she was OK? Shame it meant he would miss out on the vote and The Left would preserve their domination of Baby Labor. Now, call me soft, but I thought this sucked. Gough would have called me a virgin for being squeamish but I did not volunteer and from that day found that, sadly, I could not throw myself into the Party as I had planned. I drifted away again.

I steered clear of politics for the rest of my time on campus which was interrupted by time out for aimless back-packing and hitching around the country along with a curious detour into stockbroking (not a huge success that). But politics found me when a group of us ran for the university newspaper under the banner The Gnu Right. At the time there was much talk of the New Right in conservative political circles, fired by exciting proposals for deregulation and market reform. Anyway, we thought our dumb pun was hysterical. The Liberal Club on campus saw it as a threat. So much so that when we went to register with the student union, 'The Gnu Right' had already been lodged by the Liberal Club, just to prevent us from using the name. I'm sure the fact that Joe Hockey, future Treasurer of this country, was involved in the Liberal Club at the time was a mere coincidence. Had I any evidence I would only be too happy to accuse that colossal mediocrity of this crime. Many from that era regret that Joe hadn't stayed asleep in the plate of chips and gravy he face-planted into one lunch time at Manning Bar. He may or may not have been wearing a toga.

In short I gave politics a wide berth until middle age. By this time, after an obscure and uneventful work-life as a lawyer, working mainly in the glamorous high-octane world of credit unions and community banking, I got drawn back in. Among other things, the major parties made it a crime to report the suspected abuse of refugees and asylum seekers in camps on Manus island and Nauru. I'm sentimental about certain things and that includes copperplate handwriting and the Rule of Law. It's a nebulous concept but at its heart it protects fundamental human rights like freedom from arbitrary detention, equality before the law and the right to speak up when crimes are being committed. Stuff like that. More specifically, when we hold people in custody I think it's important that if nurses and doctors see people suffering and being abused they are able to report that to the media or police. In a free society we should be able to talk that out in public, with full knowledge of the facts. Call it whistleblowing. Or basic bloody decency. But the major political parties did not see it that way and banned our nurses and doctors from reporting abuse. That law has been repealed but we should never forget it existed. And I certainly don't — because that's why I joined the Greens. Briefly. Granddad would've been horrified!

After joining I offered to go door knocking, thinking, if we are to make a difference, this rising political force — as I saw it at the time — needs my support. So I was prepared to leaflet for the Greens at election booths and head into the streets with a clipboard to register voters. I received my training and was told my first task was to clarify whether the citizen I was talking to was in fact a Green voter. 'Why's that,' I asked. 'I thought we were into democracy and wanted voters to enrol, as a thing in itself?' The organiser said: 'yeah, nah, we want Green voters'. That troubled me. I said 'you know, we should be signing up everyone we can and then winning the fight for their vote'. The organiser was unimpressed. At the risk of being parochial I didn't like that the organiser seemed to be from outside our community when there were dozens of locals who could have done the job. In any event, the party struck me as a greener version of the bigger parties and I just did not like it. So I drifted away again . . . that was 2016. By the way, since my membership lapsed, no one has called or emailed to ask me why or to try to win me back.

And while we're talking about the largest small party in Australia . . . I don't think the Greens appreciate how much they piss off large chunks of the population. Partly because the party and its members can come across as a little sanctimonious and preachy. At times the Greens come over more like a cult than a party. But the main reason so many think 'nah, no thanks' is the disconnect between the Greens' vision and ordinary life as it is lived by most Australians doing stressful jobs in increasingly chaotic cities. Some people across the country have detached from suburban materialism because of their personal beliefs, or because they are wealthy enough to see themselves as above it, but not nearly enough to support a substantial political force. In a time when all politics is identity politics, the Greens have not found a way for the average Australian to 'see' themselves as Green.

End of dog's leg. Moral of the story: I loved my Granddad even though he voted for the DLP and I still love Gough despite his flaws. And, not surprisingly, like many people who are interested, I have struggled to get involved in party politics. Simple. But somehow we need to get over that! Not just me. But you, too.

Gimme gimme gimme

And surprise, surprise, the fundamental problems of #auspol remain unchanged. Our fearful leader Malcolm Turnbull has come and gone. The serious business of long-term planning for the future, thinking properly about defence or energy or housing or just about anything, takes a ticket as our elected representatives squabble like seagulls over a discarded box of hot chips. Like a spoilt tennis player who makes a living without winning too often and whinges every time they get a bad call. Maybe our politics reflects a society that has become all 'gimme gimme gimme'. There is a sense of grievance among our people where there should be gratitude, a meanness that says we deserve ever more stuff. There is a weird lack of proportion in how we look at the riches we enjoy. Despite our inequality we are a wealthy country. Most Australians live in a state that kings throughout history would recognise as luxury. Louis XVI did not have a home cinema, electronic toilet or an all-wheel-drive horse and carriage with 6 cup-holders, Dolby sound system and computer-assisted parking.

Instead of relishing our wealth and prosperity, we are instead encouraged to see division. The rising tide of reactionary populism since 2016 has certainly added an uglier, nastier strain to politics here and around the world. Rather than developing a sense of responsibility for others, we are invited to see discord in our own communities. To fear the foreigner. To resent the welfare recipient. To dismiss the unionist as a thug. But if we can sidestep the media slanging match long enough we all know this basic fact of life: despite our surface differences we are all pretty much the same. Even me and the average Scientologist are basically motivated by the same things (a sobering thought). We all want something useful and meaningful to do, to love and be loved, and to enjoy a bit of free time doing something interesting or amusing. Some of us are ambitious, most of us are not, not really. Most want to live well, not compete constantly. I believe that most Australians would be content with a life that is like a social tennis match, with just enough tension or competition to make it worth leaving the house but the winning is not the real point.

But these folksy facts of life do not fire our politics. Instead we manufacture complaint. We celebrate individuals and encourage hero-worship. We forget that superstars emerge from communities. We talk about teams but only when talking sport or success in business. Our community workers, our social workers are among our lowest paid, lowest status people in the country. That tells you a lot about what we value. It's nuts. We are nuts!

We are fundamentally the same, but we are sold our differences. We are sold our birth-right to a destructive selfishness. We insist on gender difference when our chromosomes and DNA are virtually identical. We end up defending our family from a world we have allowed to be harsh. We armour our children so they can participate in this system. We build them up to thrive and then fear for their safety. We watch crap TV and pay for the privilege. We drink too much. Count the bottle shops. We are too often too timid to do what we want. And if we fail in this New World Order of Constant Competition it is our fault alone! We are, most of us, deep down, tired of the rancour. We want a shared world, one in which we can work together without making dumb jokes about bleeding hearts and hippies.

And we are distracted by difference in a different way. Difference in race and gender and sexuality. Don't get me wrong, our differences and identities should be celebrated. All the people and cultures that now make up this land and the world. Everyone should be able to choose who you want to be and do what you want to do — provided it does no harm to anyone else. Race motor cars. Change your gender. Love and marry who you want. Believe in what you like. Live your traditional culture. But we do all need to come together, living with our differences, living our Common Wealth. We need a whole that is greater than the sum of our parts. An inclusive culture is important. Our identities are important. That said, the oppression of The Not So Wealthy by The Wealthier People is not about identities or gender or culture, it is about power and wealth, and it needs to be resisted head-on.

Returning to Little Bay. Circa 2003.

In 2003, in my mid 30s, I came back to Australia after five years in the UK. I had married a Welsh woman, thanks to Shirley Bassey, Dylan Thomas and JPR Williams, and we had a son. We spent some time readjusting to life Down Under with my parents in Sydney's Little Bay, in the house where I grew up in the 70s and 80s. It was Slightly Better Than Average. But only just. Red brick. Four Bedrooms. Cape Cod Extension.

I returned to find a different Sydney. A different country. I discovered food was now something you watched on TV, instead of something you ate in front of it while watching the news, the footy or Countdown. It had become a sport. People were making three-course meals under pressure, trying to beat each other ... at food. Did Australia need more sport? Then I went for a walk down Reservoir Street and noticed a Porsche 911 parked in the driveway of a newly renovated house. An insurance sales man had moved in, all by himself. Five bedrooms. The vaulting Jay Gatsby of Little Bay. Mum and dad drove a Laser until it fell apart and we all loved the orange Datsun 180B they drove for over a decade. A Porsche 911 in Little Bay was like something from out of space. What was this bloke trying to prove? Word was even his mum thought he was a bit of a wanker.

On Saturday morning we got the papers and read *The Sydney Morning Herald*. The real estate section was half the paper. The articles seemed to assume that all readers had an investment property or five. Mum and dad never invested in one because it was 'just too risky' even though they could have afforded it. The Australian property obsession was a new thing. No one really talked property before I left for the UK and now it was like a disease. Property fever! It seemed the readers of the Herald were looking to make a killing. The property owners. The landlords. It struck me that maybe we'd become a society of winners and losers, of owners and renters. Surely not! Like so many things we hadn't stopped to consider whether this change of 'vibe' was a good idea, it was just happening and the participants seemed very keen to get into it and cash in.

People of Australia, how did we get here? How did we come to be a people obsessed with real estate and home renovations, impressed by food show competitions, salted caramel ice cream and throw cushions? How did we become a society that celebrates competition above all else. That reduces the question of equality to merely being alive. If a person was breathing and finished school, then you had a chance at life, which was all that was owed to you. You could complete the entry form in the New Rat Race of Australian Life and that was that. Equality of Opportunity was all that mattered and the Outcome is up to you. Never mind that equal opportunity was still a cruel fantasy for many — to point out that home truth was 'being negative'. Everywhere and Everything said: Compete, Consume and do all it for yourself, by yourself. You are great! You. You. You. Government was crap and expensive. Tax cuts were necessary to allow us to invest in more property and even more throw cushions. More salted caramel ice creams. Unions and workers were lazy and had to be controlled. Companies were cool and groovy and needed to be looked after or they might invest overseas and not give us jobs. And on and on and on!

Bastille Day

At La Perouse Primary School in the 70s we would go to the monument every Bastille Day to sing the Marseillaise. For six weeks in 1788 the scientific expedition of La Perouse stopped on the north side of Botany Bay. We were nearly a country of the croissant. The French even met up with Phillip and the First Fleet but took off for the Pacific where they perished. The boats weren't found for over a century.

So, on July 14, kids from families who came from Malta and Croatia, Scotland and Italy, Serbia and Poland, along with some who'd lived in the area for thousands of years, gathered together to sing the great song of freedom, the world's finest national anthem. We loved singing it, even though the bit that goes 'qu'un sang impur . . . abreuve nos sillon / may the furrows of our fields flow with the blood of the impure' is a decidedly weird thing to ask nine and 10 year old kids to sing.

A great memory, though. None of us French, singing in a language we didn't know, as loud as we could, full of finger buns and chocolate milk. Kids from all corners of the world at a school where a third of the students were from indigenous families. Unusual for Sydney. For Australia. We could sing well enough but were unbeatable at rugby league. Never lost a game of football during my years at the school. And I only touched the ball a few times a game. I scored one lousy try in four seasons — a lucky intercept — but can remember it like I scored it this morning.

In July 2018 I was thinking of our Bastille Day ritual, when the nation started hearing about so-called 'Sudanese gangs' on the streets of Melbourne. Sad, angry, stupid talk. And we had idiots on steroids with flags around their shoulders on TV, talking up hate of all kinds. Meanwhile two young Sudanese men with accents as broad as their shoulders were playing Aussie Rules football at the highest level. Majak Daw for North Melbourne and Aliir Aliir for Sydney. After one game they were interviewed together on the ground. They both had blinders. Aliir, a defender, had somehow kicked the winning goal. Amazing stuff! The television station understood the meaning of the moment. As did the AFL. A moment where the Code could say it had won the battle of Australian sport. Look at these blokes. Daw, from Khartoum. Aliir, born in a refugee camp in Kenya. Stars of our game. Champions. Superstars! In the finest Aussie tradition. And not a single politician hit the screens to mention the moment afterwards. A missed opportunity. A staggering fail. Not one politician mentioned it. Wow!

Metaphors are our Salvation!

#Auspol is a joke. We need to wake up and change. We need a politics that sees Australians as people with different lives and communities but common interests that come together in a public space. And we need new metaphors to reach people. A Ministry of Metaphors might be an idea! Here is my first contribution to our National Inventory of Metaphors . . .

This exercise was tested in my show 'Alternative Prime Minister'. It was most people's favourite bit. It's humorous but deadly serious. It starts with the Venn diagram. The one thing most of us remember from maths at school. Two circles that overlap with a joiny-up bit in the middle. You have 2 kinds of Venn Diagram. Resting and Active. Behold!

Resting Venn Diagram — Here the two circles are apart with no Joiny-Up Bit.

Active Venn Diagram — Here the two circles come together to make a Joiny-Up Bit.

Why are we talking Venn Diagrams?

The circles are our Private Lives. Our homes, beliefs, wardrobes, record collections and backyard pools. Good and lovely things. The Joiny-Up Bit is our Common Wealth. Our public buildings, legal system, libraries, national parks and municipal pool. The joiny-up bit is technically called the empty set, but let's not get lost in annoying detail.

If you squeeze the Joiny-Up Bit, making it smaller due to death by a thousand tax cuts, that reduces our Common Wealth. But if you grow the Joiny-Up Bit, our Common Wealth expands. It's like we're dilating the cervix of our nation. Everyone wins, everyone is happy. As a country we need to grow the Joiny-Up Bit. Dilating the cervix of our nation is our path to redemption, to rebirth. To get the full impact of this Practical Metaphor, you need to try it yourself.

You will need two people and two hula hoops.

1. Make a Venn diagram by getting your fellow humans to bring the two Hula Hoops together so they overlap, creating the Joiny-Up Bit.
2. Look at one of the circles. Call it Your Circle. Say: 'hello circle you are my private life'. Make a list of its contents: your home, beliefs, playlists, wardrobe and backyard pool. OK?

3. Push the circles in to make the Joiny-Up Bit. That represents our Common Wealth. Our public buildings, legal system, libraries, parks and municipal pool. Our shared life not our private one. Say: 'Hello Joiny-Up Bit. You are our Common Wealth'.

4. Breathe. Relax. Take it all in.

5. Push the circles apart, making the Joiny-Up Bit smaller. Watch it shrink to a miserable rump. Say: 'That's what Death by a Thousand Tax Cuts looks like. And Everybody Hurts' (By the way, the worst song REM ever recorded).

6. Push the circles in again, making the Joiny-Up Bit bigger and bigger. Breath and relax. Behold! Watch Our Common Wealth growing and growing.

7. Approach the Joiny-Up Bit and put your hands through the gap, follow with your head and then your entire body.

8. With a flourish then say in a loud, clear voice: 'I am dilating the Cervix of the Nation!'.

You might like to draft a Metaphor or two of your own. Go on, have a crack!

Final word for this section

People of Australia, our metaphors can liberate us, teaching us the lessons we need to learn. We need to invest in the municipal pool of this country, to dilate the cervix of the nation. Then we can renew our claim to be egalitarian. With our Common Wealth in our hearts and minds and streets and communities. We need to come together to do this. I am not arguing for a socialist paradise. We'd never get there. I am arguing for a rebalancing, an adjustment. We do not need maximum profits. We need Slightly Better Than Average profits. We need to rediscover that government is important. We need to build up the things we own and do together. The detail will take ages to work out, as the tide turns away from the era of reflex tax cuts and privatisation.

We can make an Australia like an endless swimming carnival where everyone gets a go, where there's a race and a job for everyone. Sure, we have the stars who get the medals, but the old couple doing the barbecue always go home with a few bob in their pocket feeling good about themselves too. As a kid I did the races that went across the pool. And I'm OK with that. Let's go! Everyone is welcome. If we try hard enough we might one day be able to Make Australia Slightly Better Than Average Again™.

PART EIGHT:
It's the economy, drongo!

I did economics at uni. We were taught by Frank Stilwell and Ted Wheelwright, well-known political economists of the day. The famous public intellectual John Kenneth Galbraith came to visit in 1984 and lectured us on the coming 'revolution in bureaucracy'. The great social democrat thought we were drowning in paper and needed to be saved from a deathly risk aversion. What on earth would he think today? Anyway, my point here is that I have always loved economics and still read as much as I can. For mine, Ross Gittins is a greatly under-appreciated national treasure. An old-fashioned rational analyst with his eye squarely on the public interest. For those who think economics is a science, I see it more as a way of imagining and understanding our society. Our concepts of economics are fundamental to how we see ourselves as humans. So this whole section, peppered with jokes, is about economics. Because to paraphrase that great neo-liberal and progressive disappointment, President Bill Clinton, and his telling line on politics, 'It's the Economy, Drongo!'

The Black Box of the Economy

Well, derr, so much of our politics is about The Economy. Or money. Virtually every announcement made by a politician is about the money spent or allocated. You know the drill . . . someone appears in a suit, a hi-vis vest and a hard hat to say: 'we are delighted to announce we are spending $235 million on a new highway. Forty-seven million on a roundabout. Four and a half billion on a brand new port over the next 112.5 years.' The NBN or the NDIS or Gonski. And so on. It's as if the only measure of policy — or government — is that money is being spent on something. It's often the last we hear of it, too. Unless government is magically forced to admit to a budget blowout. Meanwhile every teacher, nurse and ambo has to fill in reporting forms longer than Game of Thrones every day, to justify their meagre wages. Elsewhere, ministers have replaced policy on The Economy with simply talking it up. Like encyclopaedia salesmen on an old American TV show. Like they are afraid the sky will fall in if they don't. Actually, they do this precisely because the sky will fall in if they don't. That really is economic policy now: 'Shop! Please, shop. We're begging you, shop or the game is up!'.

But here's the kicker, the killer, the crux of it all. Even though just about everything is about The Economy, no one knows how it works any more. Especially not economists. Certainly not politicians. Globally the show has been kept going by zero interest rates but only just. No one ever stops to ask why investment hasn't been going gangbusters when interest rates have been so low. Why isn't employment booming? Why aren't wages surging? Now rates are going up again and no one can say exactly why this is happening either. The program of printing money, known by the euphemism Quantitative Easing, has had its day and needs to be cancelled. There are no rules or laws to economics worthy of the name. But one thing about The Economy is clear. Any talk of a free market is a wild exaggeration. We are still in the GFC-bailout recovery phase. And the last phase of the carbon era. Both industries rely on massive support from the public purse, from government bank guarantees and QE or subsidies and policies to suppress the growth of renewables. Not to mention how arms manufacturers are financed by the Citizens of our so-called democracies in the wealthy and not so wealthy countries of the planet.

If we're honest, the Economy is an impenetrable black box and we should open it up. We are right to talk of The Post-Truth Era. It's also post-Economics. We have a global economic system where money flashes across borders at light speed, huge cash-flows zip across the planet on websites and in the dark web. No one knows what is going on or tries to control it. Instead of adjusting the affairs of the powerful to help the toiling majority in rich countries and poor, the disasters among the wealthy are bailed out by the people. You could not make up the mendacious nonsense that is the political and economic history of the last generation — no one would believe it. The Wealthier People run The Economy for themselves. So maybe it's not a black box at all. Maybe the lack of investment, the lack of real jobs and wages growth is just down to the decisions made by boards and CEOs, hedge funds and entrepreneurs everywhere to look after their interests and shareholders rather than workers and the society they operate within. Could that possibly be so?

Let's look at the facts of some crucial issues. Like housing. Home ownership has fallen during my lifetime. Once around 70 per cent it has fallen to 60 per cent. 30 years ago nearly 60 per cent of 25 to 34 years olds owned their own home, now it is down to 45 per cent; 35 to 44 years olds have fallen from 73 to 61 per cent. You would expect a country of undeniable prosperity to be maintaining or increasing the ratio. We are talking so many thousands of families and billions of dollars. But our politicians seem pretty content with this trend. Home ownership used to be something everyone agreed on as a good thing:

people should be able to buy a home. Robert Menzies took it seriously. So did every government until the 1990s. At the same time we used to invest in housing for low-income workers. But all this has changed. Why? Surely not because we thought it was a business opportunity for The Wealthier People with access to credit who could rent out their properties to people who couldn't afford to buy or had no government-funded options anymore. Government policy on housing has been a disaster for a generation and we get lost nit-picking over negative gearing tax deductions. The issue is simpler: where are We The People going to live and why can't we buy a bloody house?

Meanwhile, the price of an average degree is around the annual starting salary of a graduate, or more. Is that cool? And in the big cities, there is nowhere to rent while studying at uni. I always assumed that being able to pay your way through two degrees with a casual job in a pub or driving a cab was normal. It turned out to be a bizarre aberration in human history. My generation was incredibly lucky to enjoy the privilege. The shifts we did at the Native Rose Hotel supported two nights at the Trade Union and the Hopetoun and a day or two on the books. A privilege. We all know Labor started the trend to pay-as-you-learn education but was it ever meant to end up like this? Surely not. Better ask John Dawkins and Paul Keating. Anyone got their numbers? The point is that we have chosen a different way of life, of education, of housing; none of it is natural or inevitable.

At the same time, unemployment is now measured very differently from when Keith Windshuttle wrote his imaginatively entitled *Unemployment in Australia* way back in 1979. If a person was unemployed then that meant that they did not have a full-time job generally sufficient to support a family. Now a person is regarded as employed so long as they do an hour's work collecting supermarket trolleys in Port Augusta. If Young Jack collects trolleys for 10 hours she's categorised as an emerging leader. Perhaps the new method is used to obscure the lack of work available for ordinary people, especially the old, the young and the poor. Especially in regional Australia. We are being lied to about unemployment and underemployment. We have so much excess human capacity, so much need for work, it is on the wrong side of funny altogether.

I could go on like this but I don't want to depress you. Our first step in rebuilding our Common Wealth is to get back to talking about this stuff instead of the toxic politics of personalities and partisan mud-slinging. Who cares whether a certain politician is schtooping a schtaffer? Although it is tempting to ask how on earth the most unrootable man in #auspol history managed to cause a sex ban to be applied to cabinet ministers. But why does the ban apply to some politicians but not others? It does your head in. Who are the Tigers playing this week? What's the price of Tapis today? Anyone? Help me out. It's enough to make you turn to drink or shopping.

Politics used to be mainly about The Economy but in a very different way. That was when the Government had a sporting chance to influence it, because its policies were relevant to what companies did, it influenced wage levels and employed heaps and heaps of real workers doing so many of the things in The Economy. We can forget that very easily. In those days, if the government could keep unemployment, interest rates and inflation under 5 per cent it was said you could not lose office. Well, tell that to Julia Gillard. It was a long time ago that this rule applied, to be frank. Now that we have unwound the Government's role in The Economy we languish in puerile short-term debates with long-term consequences. Wander around a shopping centre in the outer suburbs of our capital cities and ask yourself how exciting it must be to be a barely educated 21 year old with no job and a useless degree or diploma at the mercy of The Market.

The Economy called Australia

Despite no one understanding economics anymore, The Economy is Everything. So much so that I like to say that Australia is an Economy that used to be Country. And a tiny one. We have a small population of 25 million, around the size of a Chinese city like Shanghai. Yet we do not see ourselves like that. We see ourselves as special and unique. That we're a mere shard among 7 billion never enters into our conversations. You would have thought we had a moral obligation to carry our fair share of the human load.

Australia is still very wealthy by any measure, right up the top of all the league tables for standard of living and quality of life, despite our problems. We are literate, healthy and wealthy compared to the rest of the world. Most of us have a truly incredible standard of living. Yet with all the whingeing about money and NAPLAN results in our politics you would think we all lived in a cave and that no one reads anything except faded copies of Mad Magazine, Dolly and Tracks.

The Economy is built on Mining, Banking and of course Shopping. I'm being satirical here, but not much. Mining involves pulling minerals out of the ground (with really big trucks), as well the land (which we call farming), and even our rivers (we call this water management). Banking is the national sport of transferring wealth from poorer to wealthier people through home lending, financial planning and other forms of lawful misappropriation. The size of our banking sector relative to the whole Economy — and our stock market — should worry politicians who are serious about the future of The Country. But we don't talk about that. Meanwhile, Shopping is the pastime that fills in our time between work and television because there is only so much sport you can watch. There are other things in The Economy — agriculture is an example (think buffalo mozzarella and smoked salmon). Or manufacturing, though that's pretty much down to a bloke making dolls from recycled tractor tyres on the west coast of Tassie. He has 17 per cent of the Albanian doll market. Globalisation rocks!

But, earnestly, if you asked a politician to explain how Our Economy works they would struggle to give you a proper answer. One that might convince the judges on, say, Shark Tank or Australia's Got Talent. Or one that shows why they were elected to parliament, why their party put them forward, why We The People should trust them with our lives. Conservative politicians dribble on about jobs and growth as if their actions have much to do with these things nowadays. Labor politicians pretend new hospitals and penalty rates for baristas can solve everything. And the Greens kinda yeah, nah, but yeah, pretend The Economy doesn't exist. Because the planet is sick! No kidding. The answers we are given by our representatives would not pass the pub test. They would fail the Year 9 commerce assignment test. And the bar could not be much lower than that.

A Word on Growth

Our economy is designed to grow and grow and grow. Like Edelweiss. Growth is what we want The Economy to do. Maybe to make it sound like gardening. But it's not like gardening. There's no planting. No pruning. It's weird that we focus on growth because when you study economics you get told that the subject is about satisfying unlimited human needs and wants with scarce resources — an entirely different thing from growth, growth and more growth. Our Economy has allegedly grown for longer than anyone can remember. Possibly since the time Uluru was formed. We are told that growth is the point of everything but it's not.

The real point about The Economy is this. This explains government (in)action. Nothing is allowed to change that does not suit The Market because that hurts the Economy. Got it? It's like The Economy is a highly sensitive creature, a drippy milksop with a glass jaw dressed in a Pikachu onesie on Be Like A Pirate Day. The Economy must not be tampered with, see? Proper taxation of companies or real estate investors is not a good idea. No way! Shifting subsidy from carbon to renewables is no good (well, it's not even discussed). Changing anything is just not possible. Because The Market tells us it might damage Growth. And it does so in a serious voice at the end of the news when they do the share market reports. Subsidies for privileged businesses like banks and transport companies cannot be re-directed to other parts of The Economy that might meet other objectives like, for example, public transport or renewable energy. They just can't. Because changes would hurt The Economy. And who tells us this? The Market. I know this is a bit unfair on investors in renewables but they have been shouted down for decades by more powerful voices in The Market, haven't they?

Why do we need to protect Growth? Well, the Market tells us with the calm of a parent reading Thomas The Tank Engine to a four year old that The Economy does not like shocks. And all change is a shock. By shocks The Market means risks or downsides, sudden movements or unlit car parks. Shocks to wealth and power. The Market does not like them because shocks are too much like Real Life as experienced by Not So Wealthy People. The Market likes labour market reform, tax cuts and technology that reduces costs for business including robots. They are good for Growth. But the Market does not like shocks. Ever. Got that? Meanwhile the Not So Wealthy are expected to believe a whole bunch of crap in order to get a job or promoted. You are asked to believe wealth will trickle down from up above. That the crumbs will fall from the table. If it hasn't worked out for you, that's because you have just not worked hard enough, not been positive enough, not developed the right skills at the right university (in courses you probably couldn't afford in the first place). These are the 'truths' that The Market and The Wealthier People who run The Economy expect the Not So Wealthy to believe.

Growth is not groshorhandwth but a euphemism for the status quo.

Jobs and Stuff. Unions and What Not.

While The Not So Wealthy scrabble a living in the misery machine of The Economy, The Wealthier People get on with the job of rewarding companies for sacking people or replacing them with machines. This has been a key theme of The Economy for my entire adult life. No company has ever been punished by The Market for laying people off. Take as much time as you like to think of a company that wasn't rewarded with a higher share price for cutting staff. There may be odd exception for growing companies but generally The Market says grow a pair, you hard-headed business types, get rid of some people and you can have a chocolate star. Yes, the reward for The Not So Wealthy who have made this country and The Economy is the opportunity to retrain, not an opportunity many of The Wealthier People are looking for.

Meanwhile workers can no longer go on strike unless they have a note from their mum. Companies are allowed by law to put heaps of people on labour hire contracts so they are not given the benefits enjoyed by employees. Because of Market Forces, which is shorthand for the market forces you to do this so the company gets the money and the worker doesn't. Executives meanwhile get huge pay packets for the same reason — Market Forces. Their salaries soar often when their companies aren't even doing well. The argument put by The Market is that there is a shortage of talent in the upper echelons. But we have loads of people who could run our major companies — educated people prepared to say anything to shareholders and the media in order to be paid millions. The Market will pay CEOs huge sums as long as they keep sacking people and making profits. Meanwhile, we give loose change to small businesses and entrepreneurs who take genuine risks. Our military contracts go overseas. Our super funds invest in American shopping malls rather than in our infrastructure. Why? It's all so bloody confusing and no one even tries to explain the whole picture to the people. Do they? It's almost like the incoherence of it all suits the parties that run the show. Now that couldn't be true could it?

We also value the wrong things and we know it. How can we say that a real estate agent deserves to be paid commission when flogging a hugely valuable physical asset such as a house when a nurse gets paid a meagre hourly rate for the trivial business of looking after our health? Why do we say good on you to sports and entertainment stars who get paid massive sums for doing what they love to do? While most professionals in their industries struggle to make a living. Why do we say congratulations to people who build up property empires taking rent from fellow humans who just want somewhere to live? Why do companies underpay their staff? I really don't know.

Unions might be struggling to be relevant in a gig economy and they have their issues — but the need for organising labour and the fight for workplace justice is real and urgent again.

And now for a Bit of Evidence Based Thinking and History

The Economy, like politics, is whatever you can make it. There are no real laws of The Economy. Not like physics, for example, or cricket. There are human decisions. Heaps and heaps of human decisions. And you can see what those decisions are in the world around you: the skyscrapers, houses, malls, freeways, factories, universities, churches and swimming pools. They are The Economy, not some abstract verbiage and graph series from a dusty old textbook on equilibrium, export markets and market pricing. Every generation makes the mistake of ignoring history then goes on and repeats it. Currently we are reprising the economics and politics of the period around the Great Crash of 1929. The economics of austerity and politics of reactionary populism.

The facts and faces are different and it has an entirely different quality in our online, spectacle consumerist, globalised world — but gee, we could learn something from history if we felt like it. Namely, a detached government that leaves our fate to The Market has never worked in crisis. But the longer term lesson is there is no reason we cannot remake everything we currently take for granted in politics, government and economics. The way we treat The Economy now is not how we ran it in the second half of the twentieth century, when the societies of the west experienced unprecedented growth and sharing of power and wealth. Things do change and can change again, profoundly, if we want them to.

Our Surrender to The Market

If our political class across my adult life had a theme tune it would be like the song from The Lego Movie. You can sing it now to yourself: 'everything is awesome, everything is cool when you're part of a team, that sold everything off that took ages to build up from the work of the workers and the tax of the taxpayers'.

A theme you may have picked up in this book is that our political class has surrendered The Economy to the Market through privatisation, outsourcing, deregulation, unfunding services and tax cuts for companies and individuals. In the process Government has undermined its ability to do what it is supposed to do: provide services, and to develop assets and institutions in the interests of people. But the political class of this country, like those of other western democracies, now believes politics should make Government as small as possible and get out of the way of The Market. Government is seen as a necessary evil to be minimised; the contract manager for a network of outsourcing arrangements that used to be handled directly by the public service.

We privatised electricity and were surprised to find that prices went up and not down — and destroyed communities in the process. We outsourced major infrastructure projects and were alarmed when costs blew out and out; and that the tolls on our roads only go north. We opened up tertiary education only to see many local students priced out of the uni market and dodgy operators appear from everywhere, luring vocational students with the promise of a laptop, only to be taught by staff who didn't know how to turn one on. We wound up the Commonwealth Employment Service and contracted out to so-called non-profits, who make their living out of training people for work that is not there and sending them to interviews for jobs they can't do. We outsourced refugee management to poor countries with little infrastructure because on a continent the size of Australia there was just nowhere to put anyone.

Meanwhile our banks, once over-regulated, were allowed to make as much money as they could from everything they could — insurance, financial planning, currency — by putting profit before people every hour of every day. It suited our governments because banking was profitable and profits meant dividends and rising share prices for our shareholder class and superannuation funds. Bank staff were paid more if they took more risks, if they made more money for the bank, even if they cheated people. Yes, we cheered on the banks just as we cheered on rising house prices as an inherently good thing. Superannuation is the great mixed blessing of our society, providing for people's retirements, but at the same time effectively outsourcing pensions and removing huge lumps of capital from direct investment in infrastructure and public assets — our Common Wealth. The system ties us all into the fate of the Market whether we like its ways or not.

Who knew that once we encouraged our banks to maximise profits that they would start ripping people off? Our Royal Commission into the banking industry apparently 'uncovered' widespread and serious wrongdoing across the market. The common denominator is that the major banks' boards, managers and staff were focussed on maximising profits rather than acting in the interests of customers. This is not news to people who know how banks and other big companies do business if we let them. Many executives and directors claim to be surprised when banks are caught doing the wrong thing but they're only doing what they were encouraged to do by the culture of The Economy, set by our political class and supported every step of the way by The Market. The root of our problems are cultural and structural. Over-charging, bad advice and charging dead people only occurs if you are committed to maximising profits and there is no real risk of penalty.

Yet nothing will fundamentally change now despite widespread outrage. The odd rogue will be purged. But no bank will lose its licence. It's as if it is unthinkable that our regulators would ever use their power to actually properly punish a bank. Let's not forget that the first bank to cop a belting — AMP — sacked its Chairperson and appointed the man who for years ran the biggest bank, the ironically named Commonwealth Bank. David Murray more or less designed the whole system of unfettered profit maximisation. And AMP was a case study of the change in Australia. What was originally a boring but useful and valuable mutually-owned insurance company became a psychotic profit-hungry disaster of a bank. You wouldn't read about it. But you can: in the alarming and entertaining transcripts of the Royal Commission.

But again, I have to point out that We The People have generally applauded as our politicians sold off public assets to the Market, to release the value in banking, electricity, telecommunications, prisons, education and employment services. Even social security debt recovery and land title registries — key government functions or services, have been outsourced, for god's sake. Really boring stuff that is tailor-made for the public service and public ownership. We have not really voted for any of that. None of that back-office stuff gets discussed while we're bewitched by leadership speculation and the latest scandal about nothing much.

Telstra, Qantas, CBA, the CES, even Medibank Private . . . all flogged off. The new NDIS is already generating complaints because the system was designed to replace government services based on faith rather than evidence. We have surrendered control over so much. And for what? We have let accountability fly to the winds. We are reduced to screaming at call centre staff complaining about the cost of electricity and mobile phone plans, the very things we privatised to enjoy the efficiencies and competitive benefits of The Market. Cheaper prices. Yeah, right! Maybe we privatised all these things so we could enjoy the superior complaints management systems of the private sector? Help me out here . . .

Here's one thing you will never hear from the political class: let's have a royal commission into the success of privatisation of public enterprises and assets by federal and state governments over the last 40 years or so. You will not hear that because it will expose the dead set rip-off that has been perpetrated on the people of this country. Communities have been dismantled. Livelihoods are insecure. Workplaces are less safe. The Not So Wealthy are worse off. The Wealthier People are better off. To be frank, it's a mild version of what happened in Russia after the Soviet Union collapsed when the state businesses were sold to the Oligarchs in a fire sale. Except no one here has the balls to do business like Putin. So in Australia the spoils are spread among the top 10 or 20 per cent of the country instead of the top 10 individuals. Yes, The Wealthier People here are, arguably, a bunch of poor man's Putins. You might like to make that point at your next staff meeting, annual general meeting or performance review. Let me know how you get on.

Short Memories and The Bribe of Tax Cuts

Australia has forgotten how we built this country. We built banks and railways, phone companies and hospitals and libraries and showgrounds. Like the entire world around us. How did it all get there? Did Joyce Mayne or Bert Newton run a telethon? Did L. Ron

Hubbard pluck them from the sky? No, we passed around the akubra, the terry towelling hat or the beanie, and we paid for them ourselves. Some private capital but lots of public coin. Mainly through taxation supported by a few sausage sizzles and the odd chook raffle or lottery. We chipped in like Australians. Like people who like to do things together. For each other.

But we don't do that now. And why? Because tax cuts. Because, it was decided by our elected officials that The Market did everything better. In pushing this idea no one ever talked about how this meant our Common Wealth would slowly shrink and government would lose control of how things work across society. What story were we told about privatisation? Only the upside, the anticipated benefits of releasing the value and none of the downside.

Meanwhile, We The People have been bought off with Tax Cuts. A shiny trinket dangled to distract us from the gradual undermining of government itself and the ever growing power of companies. Tax Cuts may give us nominally more money in our pockets but only to pay for things that are heaps more expensive than they used to be. Do the maths. We might pay less tax but pay so much more in rent or mortgage payments and power or phone bills. Do a little calculating before the kids come home. The story of the last generation is that We The People have lost control of the Economy. The profits of the new economic activity go to the private owners and not the people as a whole, and prices go up and tax cuts don't make up the difference. Awesome!

In short, Tax Cuts are an opportunity to pay tax to someone new. Instead of paying tax to the government you pay a new tax in the form of higher house prices, higher mortgage or rent payments, power bills and whatever you buy at Westfield. And so on. The Privatised Economy Tax. In a culture only to happy to load you up with debt so you can compete with your neighbours. Consider this: if you are a teacher with five years' experience and have saved every dollar of your wages since graduation you cannot buy any property east of Parramatta in Sydney. Not even if you lived on bananas and water crackers, and had a second job working nights as an artisanal actuary on Airtasker. You couldn't scrounge the deposit let alone qualify for a mortgage. Even if your partner had the same job. You would need help from your parents, or armed robberies. My father was a teacher and bought a home in Kingsford using only his salary. The same person in the same job could not do that in the same part of Sydney today. Given this basic fact of life, how can we say Australia has been well governed and is a better place than it was?

I do not understand why people cop Tax Cuts. Apart from anything else, the amounts involved are tiny. It is a modest bribe, a short con. Further, there is no country on earth where corporate tax cuts have been demonstrated to deliver jobs. Instead companies tend to keep shedding jobs after they get tax cuts. And why is that? Because there is no obligation for companies to be grateful. At the same time, incentives to cut costs, namely, people's jobs, remain intact because shareholders love short term profits. The Market loves it too because boosting revenue takes loads more effort than cutting costs. It's almost like instead of being creative risk-takers, business folk are mostly flat-track bullies who take the soft option every time.

To be clear, as we all know, both major parties support tax cuts. Yet they are a cancer to our social democracy. Australia is already a low tax country. But our political class doesn't want you to know or consider that, because they want government to be as small as possible. No progressive party worthy of the name should support tax cuts. Incidentally, for the policy nerds, property supremacists, like the libertarian economist James Buchanan, author of The Calculus of Consent, are relevant to this debate but aren't the source of the problem. The long history of deregulation in Australia starts not with conservatives but with the parties of organised labour who began this process 35 years ago, after the conservatives bottled it. The real results are only now being felt. We have redesigned our culture very quickly and not drawn breath to think it all through. Must be something in the water. But don't start me on water, our most fundamental natural resource and public asset . . .

What we don't talk about when we talk about tax cuts . . .

Heaps of stuff! Let's be clear that we now have a long-term trend towards robots and automation that is really reducing jobs. It's such a big deal you'd think politicians would be keen to talk about it and to reassure people that plans are in place. No way! Because they have no policies for dealing with this massive social change. None. Because any policy would require seriously heavy lifting, complex thinking, consultation, imagination and money. That is to say, taxation or at least changing things around a bit. It would involve what used to be called Government. And the idea that it is the job of Government to tell a story about the future and to plan for it. Much easier to bang on about terrorists, refugees and immigrants, cutting spending to keep The Market happy and bribing the punters with Tax Cuts (while destroying social democratic government along the way).

Talking tax cuts also means we are not discussing budget priorities. An alarmingly bi-partisan area of non-debate is defence spending. Government spending will always be cut except when it comes to the defence budget — or as we might more accurately describe it Citizen crowd-funding of the military-industrial complex. Money is always found for the hardware of war and the machinery of fear — from airport security to new laws on espionage, new uniforms for our Border Force and especially for new weapons for our armed services such as drones and submarines. I am not saying we should defend ourselves with feather dusters but we should talk about how and why we spend all this money when our schools and roads and hospitals and public transport need work and there are so many other things that every single cent that goes to the military could be spent on. Why are the major parties at each other's throats on literally every issue except defence spending? And what use are 12 or 15 or 20 submarines going to be if we get attacked? I know how big the northern coastline of Australia is. Massive. I had 15 submarines playing battleships with my sister as a kid and I couldn't defend my end of the bathtub where I sat with my back to the taps! How is such a modest array going to defend Darwin, Port Headland and Weipa?

Tax. What's in it for business?

A final word on tax. Tax cuts, some say, are about returning money to the people because — as conservatives say — the money is ours. Well, that's debatable. All the profits made by companies and the wages earned by individuals are the result of a complex chain of interdependence because we humans exist in a web of collective activity. All companies rely on workers to generate revenue and profits and could not do what they do without a huge array of publicly-funded infrastructure to support them. This needs to be said. And again and again. From roads to ports, from schools to telecommunications. It's a bit embarrassing to recite these obvious things. But no one ever talks about them. Even if a lot of our infrastructure — like ports — is now privately, even foreign, owned — much of it was built by the government. Not to mention the array of subsidies and policies that also support companies across The Economy. Like public hospitals and schools with good buildings and well paid staff, like roads and public transport. Like medical research and effective regulation of our economy and protection of our environment. All that wild and crazy stuff. Yes, our business community, our chambers of commerce, our entrepreneurs fledging and established, all benefit from a strong public sector. Where on earth do we think the research behind solar power, wireless internet and cochlear implants happened? In a conservative think-tank? At Gina Rinehart's Christmas party? Out the back of the leagues club after trivia night? No, in publicly-funded universities and research facilities.

The Vision Thing

And while I've got your attention, what is government's vision for our industries? We used to talk about that, too. As adults. As a country. Now it's just jobs and growth, or schools and hospitals, with the details left to your imagination. Because no one knows. We know the current government supports fossil fuels. A bit of a sad addiction, that. They're like guilty smokers. Maybe it's linked to the business of their major funders. That's just a theory. Like Einstein's work on relativity. Obviously you can't get rid of coal mines and the whole system that surrounds them over the course of a long weekend. There's an entire eco-system of communities and companies, of families and workers. Many people would like to think you can wish these things away, like a bad dream. But you can't. Yet you can design government policy that manages a transition from one energy base to another as is happening in other countries. You know, bat-shit-mad countries like Germany and even the United Kingdom. You can keep a little coal going, and the people it supports, while moving to a new platform of renewable energy. We can make the Harsh Aussie Sun more than a source of skin cancer and turn ourselves into a Renewables Super Power. We need to want to do it, though. We could get serious about the kind of world we leave for our kids and grandkids — you know, the people our MPs say they are in politics to do stuff for.

Successive governments have shown a fondness for saying we're not in the business of picking winners but governments pick winners all day, every day. Like when choosing old energy over new, when government subsidises diesel fuel but not the arts, when it consigns the car industry to the rust bucket of history, when it makes policies that suit the big banks but not the little ones that keep money in our communities. Or when it says gambling is OK although it knows it is a tax on people already living marginal, stressed-out lives who can't afford it. Or when it decides to spend a lot of time and money chasing alleged social security debts owed by The Not So Wealthy instead of going after Wealthier People and their tax-fiddling vehicles designed by fancy accountants. Like Derek.

Even more importantly we do not hear our leaders ever come out and say, hey, here is where we see The Economy being in 2050. This, People of Austraya, is what we hope your country might look like, if we play smart and work hard. For example, the government — whatever party it comes from — might say:

> Australia in 2050 will be a prosperous country known around the world for its strong and nimble technology companies and its high-quality new agriculture, a renewable energy super power, harnessing the natural advantage of its sunlight, a tertiary education hothouse offering free university degrees to its kids, a country that has rediscovered its love of government and building strong communities, a country that works for peace all over the Pacific and beyond.

You know, that kind of vision. Sure it sounds a bit old-fashioned, but isn't that what we're missing? Instead, we hear: 'We will become one of the top ten weapon exporting nations on earth'. Okaaaaay. Got that? Weapons. Guns, artillery, army ducks. I nearly died when that line was trotted out by the government early in 2018. Of course we already make munitions. Who doesn't love the Lithgow Small Arms Factory? But weapon exports as a growth industry? No time for renewables but weapon exports are the New Black? It turns us into a local franchise operator for the military-industrial complex. If we're exporting weapons we should start with the ones who came up with this idea. We do not need to make weapons for the Middle East or Africa or Asia to support wars that make the world more dangerous. Yet when this policy is discussed all we get are bland assurances that our weapons would only be used by good people doing good things. Sounds like something out of *Possum Magic* or *The Wiggles Go To Wollongong*. We never discuss our defence strategy and are told that we can't talk about that stuff because it is classified. We are treated like children. And that has to stop. Doesn't it?

PART NINE:
Various thoughts I couldn't fit in elsewhere

This section is for readers who might like to read a few riffs on the key themes of this book. Brain dumps. Mini-essays on background ideas. Some of it is straight and serious. Other bits are jovial. You'll work it out. But the binding theme is an interest in history, who we really are and the kind of society we would like to live in. And the issues that should influence or frame our politics and government.

Justice and Colonisation. The Long Tail of Terra Nullius.

I was 26 when the High Court of Australia abolished the legal doctrine of Terra Nullius in the Mabo case, which saw Eddie Mabo establish the right — within Australian law — to native title over Mer Island, where he and his people had lived for quite some time. Until this moment, in 1992, it was law in this country that the land was somehow empty when British colonists arrived and invaded in 1788. Despite people living all over the continent. Despite the communities. Despite the houses. Despite the middens. Despite the facts.

So the British, as they were known, arrived to establish their foreign culture here, with violence — towards each other and everyone they came into contact with — and with sustained bloodshed as happened all over the British empire. Like other empires. The British — or the Europeans as we tend to call them though there were not many Italians or Greeks or Poles involved — proceeded to build a modern society over time with incredible effort and imagination while wreaking havoc on the people who had lived here, not in emptiness but fullness, for tens of thousands of years.

In my life time, the Whitlam, Fraser and Hawke Governments came and went without Terra Nullius being overturned. Collingwood broke its long drought between flags in 1990. Crocodile Dundee made Paul Hogan famous and Strop more rich than he ever imagined, all while Terra Nullius was still law. Australia and Alan Bond won the America's Cup in 1983. So much happened before this national disgrace was reversed.

The Mabo case decided once and for all that Terra Nullius was false. That Australia was never empty land. That the locals owned it. Our law says that now. But it also means that every bit of land owned by non-indigenous people is legally owned and always has been — even though no treaty, no formal settlement, has been reached on the dispossession of the original owners. It is worth considering what Daryl Kerrigan proved in his famous legal battle in *The Castle* — that compensation on just terms must be paid when the government wants your land. If we applied that law, our various indigenous peoples, the relevant owners in 1788, would be entitled to compensation on just terms. Compulsory acquisition is always permitted by our constitution, by the way. The government has the power to take land provided it pays for it. But nothing has ever been paid.

Since the Mabo case in 1992 Australia has said sorry to the Stolen Generations; or at least, the federal government apologised to the children removed from their families. Yet even then we didn't go far enough. We congratulate ourselves for the statement Rudd made as Prime Minister in 2007 and many condemn those who did not support him on the day. But our government has never apologised to all indigenous Australians past and present. Nor have we paid a cent to compensate for the damage done and that keeps being done, which started with the land and the long lie of Terra Nullius. We need look no further than the significant over-representation of indigenous people, particularly children, in our jails and other facilities. Or the difference in life-expectancy between indigenous and other citizens. All the Marcia Langtons and Kathy Freemans, Aaron Pedersens, Bruce Pascoes, Cyril Riolis and Deborah Mailmans don't make up for the on-going wrongs that need to be righted.

After Mabo, we didn't stop and think, hey, a treaty might be a good idea at this particular moment in history. Or how about a proper sitdown and listen to what the first people have to say? Back in 1988, the Prime Minister Bob Hawke actually promised indigenous Australia a treaty at Barunga. He got excited as he tended to and then didn't follow through. Yothu Yindi wrote their song *Treaty* about Bob's broken promise. And Australia certainly didn't offer to chip in for any back rent. Not then and not ever. By 1993, as the country responded to Mabo, the pragmatics of our raw-boned, square-jawed politics, saw Prime Minister Keating making sure that farmers and pastoralists retained their right to land. Overnight the nation became experts in the nuances of pastoral leases and their ability to extinguish native title. The possibility that native title and pastoral leases might co-exist like the rights of British farmers to use and graze animals on The Commons was never fully explored. Something that had fought so hard to be born, an acknowledgment of indigenous land ownership within white man's law, was stifled from the outset.

Ending Terra Nullius and creating native title is not the end of the lie about this land that we are entitled to be here. If someone arrived today to dispossess everyone who currently regards themselves as a land owner, you can be sure the event would be remembered and bristle with 'us' for a long, long time. Centuries. As it happens, a lot of indigenous people say they do not want us to go but many do want us to say, loud and clear: this land is your land . . . we are sorry for colonisation in its entirety and its aftermath. Something like that. And I have heard it said that we need to listen above all. Who really knows what a Treaty means or might look like to indigenous communities across Australia? And as one man put it: why would I want self-determination? That is a white man's idea.

For whatever white, non-indigenous culture has achieved on this continent, as with colonists everywhere, we are the heirs to an invasion. Some say we should move on, that the troubles and the wrongs were long ago, that no one alive is at fault. Sure, the worst crimes happened long ago. The massacres. The institutionalised abuse and mistreatment. But not so long ago and not by the rhythm of time of this land and its first people. And Australia — not the name of this place when Cook or Philip arrived — is still the beneficiary of that brutality. 'We' are winners of the violent lottery of history. 'We' have had moments of kindness. 'We' have achieved great things in producing a wildly prosperous society that is exceptionally peaceful by the standards of human history and a triumph of multi-cultural harmony, for all our faults and strains of racism. But we, the colonisers, we the people of kerb and guttering, of cars and shopping centres, used our power to enrich ourselves and cause harm to the original and uncompensated owners. And we still do. Maybe that's what needs to be said. A proper sorry. And then we can start working out the details of what we can do together in a new and better way. Then 'we' can truly include all of 'us'. One day.

On Tax. History is Surprisingly Fiscal.

You would be amazed, dear reader, by how many of the Big Moments in History — how many of our Revolutions — have been about tax. Seriously. The boring question of tax and government budgets — who pays for what the state does whether good or bad — is central to so many historical dramas. For example, the English Civil War and the American War of Independence. King Charles inherited a mess from the Tudors who liked the occasional party and hunting trip but didn't much fancy running a rational bureaucracy dedicated to serving the needs of peasants and the emerging civil state. So the new King brought in a bunch of taxes he thought would fix things and succeeded only in properly pissing off the nobles who were used to enjoying an easy life (as easy as it could be in mid-millennium England without cars or electric toilets). Charlie Boy essentially said hey I'm the King and I rule by divine right so you just better do what I say and start coughing up for my Navy and fine clothes. The Nobles told him to get stuffed and after a long time mulling it over, they chopped off his head. The takeaway from this? The English Civil War — a revolution, although the English prefer not to call it one — started with tax. Exciting, huh?

A similar thing happened a couple of centuries later when England tried to pay for its dumb expensive wars in Europe by taxing the good people in the Thirteen Colonies, or the United States of America as they became known. The Americans said, 'hang on, we've been pretty busy over here opening up a new country, battling nature, warring with indigenous people, making an entire new civilisation that includes fences, roads and hot dog vans — and now you Hooray Henrys want us to pay for wars that your massive ego got you into and have 5/8 of nothing to do with us?' After this splendid speech the Young Americans muttered you're a mad bastard, Your Majesty. But King George, who certainly was mad, didn't hear them and didn't heed the lesson of King Charles. George kept his head if not his mind, but lost the American colonies way before Britain should have done. The King insisted on taxation and was prepared to go to war! Even though the Founding Fathers talked a good game about life, liberty and the pursuit of happiness, the USA is the result of a massive dummy spit about taxation.

In the world today we see tax at the centre of everything again. We are told by our politicians that companies will not invest in this country (and elsewhere) unless taxes are cut, because that way the monster of business can be coaxed into investment and create jobs for everyone. Profits are never mentioned by opponents of taxation for reasons that remain obvious at the time of publication. It is true that some countries on our planet have become tax havens or dropped corporate tax to crazy levels — mainly, if we are honest, they are countries that have little else to offer, like Ireland or The Bahamas.

Of course, the deeper truth is that taxes differ around the world and are just one part of corporate investment decisions, which anyone who spends five minutes thinking about this well knows. But the facts never deter mad people. As we are now learning (for the umpteenth time in human history), if The Wealthier People are given enough power and airtime, and the Not So Wealthy are sufficiently tired and distracted, the Wealthier People will argue that tax is theft and that they owe society nothing. Every now and then in the history of our species these ideas take root. And they are upon us again. Just as they were in the 1920s when the western world fell into a disabling depression that took ages to repair. What began in the 1980s as a correction to the inefficiencies of the bloated state and the relaxation of a rigid world of trade has ended up as a destructive lifestyle choice for the planet, driven by a philosophy that sees government as useful only for doing armies, immigration control and the ministerial car pool.

On Risk. We are Swimming Between the Flags.

Our nation of larrikins has become obsessed with risk management. Our reflex is NO. Followed by wait a bit. Then we'll see, I'll get back to you when I've spoken to the risk people. We're at the point now that you can make a joke about risk matrices over a beer with family and get a laugh because people understand it. To be honest, it's a massive risk to human happiness and our prosperity. Risk registers are the cane toads of contemporary business and government.

Don't get me wrong, we don't want people dying at work or taking dodgy medicines. We don't want people driving at 200 km/h through a strip mall or making Molotov cocktails in a camping thermos next to a school. Risk management is important, but it shouldn't be our all-purpose approach to everything in life. Most of the great achievements in history involved massive risks. From Civil Engineering to Citizen Kane to having a baby.

Above all, to develop new industries we need to explore and take risks. To support new businesses in technology, agriculture and renewables. Some of our projects will fail. And that is exactly as it should be. We Australians think we are crazy adventurous people because we go bungie jumping in Queenstown and back-packing in South America. We are not. Certainly not in business. Or in our local councils. We once built the Snowy Mountains Hydro Scheme. Now we struggle to heat a swimming pool for winter. What happened? When did we change? Or have we always been like this and not noticed? I'm confused.

As a nation we are swimming between the flags, if you like. And don't tell the lifeguards this but most of the great things in life happen outside the flags. Like surfing out the back or doing an ocean swimming race. Or back-packing in Peru or taking the river boat back through the north of Guatemala when you are told not to, point blank. But if you do, you might see a full moon rising at sunset, a tree full of cranes and meet someone you know you are going to dance with later that night.

I am not suggesting a particular policy here. I am merely suggesting we need to start working out new ways of saying YES. And not yes to miners or property developers or dodgy start-ups washing black money through venture capital firms. No, I'm talking about an attitude that says, let's stop arguing about negative gearing and the Adani mine and tax cuts for business and weapon exports as the salvation of the nation. Let's start being a country that is serious about creating a new future based on technology, agriculture and renewable energy. Let's say YES to that future. How's that sound?

On Privatisation. The Enclosures and Clearances of Our Time?

One day, the privatisations of government-owned businesses and assets in the late twentieth and early twenty-first centuries might be seen as the Enclosures or Clearances of our time. When they are happening the big events in human history always seem to have a good reason behind them. The state, as an owner of enterprises in aviation and telecommunications or mining, was slow and struggled to find capital to expand and innovate. And sometimes we would simply be ignored when we had a complaint or a simple need for service from a government instrumentality. Yet the private sector has learnt how to repeat these failures more or less perfectly.

With the enclosures in Britain the aristocracy wanted to make larger farms to take advantage of wonderful new technology and competition among other ambitious, greedy people. That is to say, the land-owning class wanted to enrich themselves. As did the Lairds in Scotland when they cleared the Highlands. Much to everyone's surprise widespread suffering ensued when the peasant lands were enclosed. And exactly the same thing happened when the Highlands were cleared. When all this happened there was no plan for the dispossessed because they did not matter. The poor had to work it out for themselves. Their lives were overthrown. No jobs to go to. No consent obtained. Dispossession has rarely been a matter of negotiation.

So, government was slow and sloppy. But in our recent privatisation fever we have ransacked utilities and banks and prisons and airlines and schools and along the way we have not merely privatised economic activities but created a new society. Our new order privileges the market and law of contract. This new order says you are on your own and competition is the value system that will shape our lives. The question is whether our smart phones and discount airlines are enough to make up for the control and the stability we have lost. Is the sense of being alone with so many shiny toys nourishing enough as a lived experience? Consider the facts. The people living on the streets or in our parks, on our beaches, in their cars. The numbers of depressed men, women and children. Those without work or enough work. We have privatised life itself. And it is no better than what we had. We have strong global brands, efficient supply chains and car-accessible discount outlets. We flock to them and pay our Privatised Economy Taxes. Whose interests does all this serve?

Fascism. Is that what we are dealing with?

People talk about fascism being upon us or parked just around the corner. I say that the word is beside the point. Sure, we can learn from the past and the horrors of the period when fascism was prominent in Europe. No one wants to see a Mussolini, Hitler, Salazar, or Franco return to high office anywhere. Nor do we want the despots of the developing world, the Pinochets and the Duvalliers, the Mobutos and the Verwoerds. For all their faults, political parties and the diffusion of power are better than autocracy.

People forget though that the current democracies of Germany and Italy and Spain were rather different places in the first part of the twentieth century from what they are today. They were not established democratic societies with mature institutions. These countries struggled then with the extreme poverty of the working class and the unresolved horrors of the first world war. They were not educated. They were not properly literate. They had barely industrialised. Cars were new. Few had fridges. There were no shopping centres.

We are educated now. We can all read. We have television and the internet. We should be able to see what is happening. Our luxury and learning should help us see even more clearly the value of our freedom and democracy. But it seems we cannot. We seem to have something new at hand. With our lives subjected to surveillance and big data monitoring. With the stirrings of the reactionary right and the acquiescence of so many in the erosion of civil liberties in the service of the so-called War on Terror. This is a completely unprecedented transformation in the nature of reality, government and democracy. We seem to have a culture of government that has dispensed with the tradition of accountability; that has made the outrageous lie the norm. We have done this at light speed. Vladislav Surkov in Russia may have started the concept of 'political theatre' under Vladimir Putin, but it is now mainstream practice across the West, with ever-multiplying stories, coming then going, sold as news to the people. Korea or Syria one minute. Kardashian and Kaepernick the next. Then . . . gone.

The sheer volume of news material is too much for anyone to absorb, let alone analyse and respond to in any coherent way. Democracy is based on information and knowledge. Informed choice among voters based on a known set of facts. This is no longer the lived reality of a democratic life. In a super literate, hyper-informed age, it has become impossible to be a Citizen. There is too much to know. Too many contested visions of too many things.

So we console ourselves with amazing cars, smart phones and tax cuts. Everything is available in salted caramel. The flavours are so good, we stay passive, wedded to our misery. We are privatised. We are consumers. We are choking on information. We are sipping vermouth. This is not fascism but a new horror that we are yet to properly name. Overpriced and terribly tasty.

Hoover and Trump

Few people alive remember Herbert Hoover. He was the President of the United States of America when the Great Depression hit. He oversaw a disaster and his career ended in disgrace. Millions of unemployed across his country and the world. People starved to death. The horrors of the times are known by all, but what few people know is that Hoover was a great man. A spectacularly successful businessman — an engineer — who used his wealth and profile for good before he entered politics. He set up some of the world's first mass welfare and disaster relief programs to save many of the people of Belgium after the Great War.

When Hoover won the White House in 1928, he had just served as an industrious and popular Secretary for Commerce. Yet four years later he was close to a pariah. He had applied the conventional prescriptions of prudence and saving, of tax and balanced budgets when the government needed to invest in its industries and people. Hoover believed in the prescriptions of Alfred Marshall and the other neo-classical economists whose theories floated serenely above the suffering of ordinary people. The lessons of Keynes were down the road. Hoover also insisted on continuing the lavish dinners at the Whitehouse; trimming his sails would have been dispiriting to the people, he thought. A rooster on election, a feather duster on his departure from office at the end of a single term.

Donald Trump is no Hoover. He lost the popular vote and squeaked into office through the weird electoral college system that determines the winner of the presidential race. A gold-toothed deal maker rather than a solid professional fellow. More huckster than humanitarian. Yet I have a sense of the shadow of Hoover approaching Pennsylvania Avenue. Millions watched Trump on television hosting *The Apprentice*. It's an oddly underrated part of his rise; noted but not weighted properly in the homeland of couch potatoes. To his fans, Trump was and remains, for many reasons, for them, the great hope of the country.

Now Trump has emerged at a time of fracture and confusion, of underemployment and industrial decline. His orthodoxy (which he would barely understand let alone believe) is the New Mistake, a weird hybrid of gangster capitalism and economic nationalism driven by the interests of an elite convinced of their right to rule, epitomised by the Brothers Koch. The anger and frustration with the dysfunctional economic order that he used to ride his way to power will likely devour him in the end. Trump, The Human Headline, has dominated our global media like no one before. He shifts and twists like a bored salesman behind on his targets doing bad coke in a Holiday Inn hotel — from Korean nukes to smashing the G7, from bombing Iran to unwinding NATO. So much attention, he almost is the global consciousness, but for what? To accelerate the pillaging of the state, the undermining of government and the service of corporate interests. If the jobs don't come and the bills aren't paid, he'll be Hoovered up by history.

For mine, there is really only one thing worth saying about Donald J Trump, 45th president of the United States of America, and that is that politics matters, that democratic institutions matter, that everyone, young, old and in-between should be interested in and get involved in politics. Another thing worth saying is that the boorish, illiberal and unjust realities of his rule should not obscure the inequity and failings of the USA before his rise to power.

Imperialism. Some say we've never come to terms with our colonial past.

We don't even talk about colonialism any more but we still behave like imperialists when we get the chance. Whenever Australia deals with PNG, Timor Leste and the Solomons, our talent for empire is on display. We lend PNG money to develop its resources to our profit, we spy on the Timorese when negotiating treaties, we play the cop in the Solomons and leave its economy open to exploitation. We ignore altogether what is happening in Irian Jaya or Bougainville. Not to mention our dealings in Nauru where we pretend a nation of 10,000 people can run its own independent government, economy and judicial system and outsource our refugee management to a dot of limestone with the population of a country town. We exploit Nauru now with detention centres as we used to when mining superphosphate there for decades.

We also remain an outpost for another Empire, just as we were back in the day. Our bases in Darwin and Pine Gap show that we remain an occupied people. Our defence budget is a tribute we pay to the military-industrial complex. But there is nothing complex about it. Not to mention our occupation of a land that was never ceded to us. So before we get carried away, let's have a little think about what imperialism means. Just because we technically don't have colonies anymore does not mean that all that stuff is over.

Participation. The Deterrence Mechanics of Machine Politics.

As we all know, a major problem or obstacle to change is the professionalisation of politics. The networks of politics were always difficult to penetrate and never really a place for the uncertain or weak.

But now the professional operators are in charge it truly is hard for the ordinary person to get involved in the business of politics.

Some of us bravely turn up to party branch meetings only to be surprised by spivs. Desperados full of passionate intensity, ready to fundraise, branch stack, troll and fight, fight and fight but for what? A chance to keep fighting it seems. Careerist functionaries like this — or amateur schemers — are an unpleasant surprise to most ordinary people. So we soon leave that arena.

In parliament we see the cream of our political parties. Like Julie Bishop. Like Tanya Plibersek. Accomplished. Stylish. Knowledgeable. Experienced. Impressive. These characters are utterly unlike the knuckle-draggers who control our political parties, who do their grubby work. Our parliamentarians are shop window dummies, the respectable face of machine politics. Up close, the better ones have an intimidating ooze about them, a sense of authority and competence. Rub up against Turnbull in the street. He's a nightmare, the embodiment of the failure of #auspol, a cuckolded husk of a politician, but in person, even when boring you to death repeating the words 'ensure' and 'Bill Shorten is a thought criminal' endlessly he will float like a crème caramel in a sugary sauce, enjoying a life without friction, insulated from full body contact with the daily realities the rest of us must endure.

It's the back-roomers, however, the car park sociopaths, the machine zealots who really run us: the knob-ends behind the scenes; the operators; the lobbyists; the funders. They enslave us in the rolling carnival of bullshit that is the daily digital newsfeed — parsing the polls and shaping the soundbites — and condemn us to the perpetual fake war of counterfeit politics where everything is hollow and fought for like nothing else matters or exists.

How divided can a country truly be that can barely disagree on who runs it? Our parties are forever neck-and-neck in the polls. Rather than confirming the division in our society, it confirms that our differences are overstated, that the parties are almost indistinguishable from each other, and that maybe the parties themselves perpetuate this state of affairs, this neck-and-neck fight because the alternative requires more effort, imagination and risk! And because they would lose their power if the rules of engagement changed . . . because they couldn't cope.

Feminism. A good idea.

When asked what he thought about western civilisation, Mahatma Gandhi, the famous leader of non-violent resistance against British imperialism, said 'what a good idea'. I feel the same way about feminism. If we are to take the idea seriously, feminism has barely begun. If by 'feminism' we mean women's liberation from the cultural predominance of men. As long as there is a fight for the right to abortion, to equal pay, to have violence towards women, especially in the home, taken seriously, then feminism remains in its infancy. Some people might find this a challenging thought. Some would say this is outrageous. Well, suck it up, fellas. When men claim to be 'disadvantaged' by feminism, they are experiencing the friction caused by the green shoots of equality. Yes, when the roots of a new plant grow in the garden — to quote Chauncey Gardener — 'chaffing may occur on the trunks of the older trees'.

Here's what I reckon. Men should look for ways to make meaning in their lives rather than worrying about holding onto the power and privilege that was traditionally given to them rather than earned. For too long women have subordinated their personal interests in order to preserve communities and families, but rather than women becoming more competitive, it's about time men did their fair share. Men could start by asking themselves simple questions like: what can I do to help another person today or how about I do something for someone who's really not going so well? That would be useful.

My Generation Says . . .

'I have worked hard and done well. I am a decent person. Not perfect. No saint. I do what's right for my kids. It's all for them. I do not covet my neighbour's wife or oxen, though I could be up for a threesome. And what happens at conferences is my business. I do community work. Judged by the standards of human history I am a good person and my success shows that our country is not perfect but basically good. Like me and my wife and my family. In saying all this, I know we might ignore the suffering of the poor, the cost of living, the stress of ordinary life, the amazing explosion of wealth and the staggering concentration of it. In short, I am a bit busy succeeding in so many areas of my life to really notice how a wealthy country can unwind so much of what was good in it and contain so much discord. But everyone is too busy to do anything about it. We're a bit too detached from each other, so busy competing and comparing that we can't get it together to change anything. I get that. It's intense you know. I do everything I can to protect my family from the society we have created. That's my job. I am committed to that. And we always organise a table for a charity night and do the snags at the footy club once a season. The overriding feeling of the country I reckon, if you look at it, which I share, is, can we just get through this so I can get home and have a glass of wine'.

Generation X. Are we to blame?

Yes. We are so ludicrously easy on ourselves. We pretend we have been dealt a dud hand. That the Boomers are to blame because they gave up on their ideals and lined their pockets. The hippies betrayed us when they straightened up. Rubbish. We the people aged between 45 and 60 are responsible for the world. In large measure and now. For its ideas and its failures. For the lack of new ideas to help salvage this culture. It is no mistake that the recent presidential candidates in the US and major party leaders in the UK are over 60. Barack Obama failed. Not all bad but terribly disappointing. There is no new movement my generation has created. There was Occupy, briefly, on the fringe of our democracies. Syrizas, Podemos and Red Star are trying to find new ways. The left in South America is withering. Macron in France won power with a new party that wrong-footed the established parties with charisma and new energy but no new ideas, in fact he is all about neoliberalism playing catch up in that country. There was Yanis Varoufakis who attained power as Greek Finance Minister, had a windmill tilt at the European establishment then resigned. There is Jacinda Ardern in New Zealand, on the outskirts of global democracy, a new-generation Helen Clark, who echoes the decent, progressive labourism from the turn of this century. A drop of sweet honey in an ocean of corporatised filth.

Our generation has not contributed much to the grand history of new ideas. We have not lined up behind a new agenda, a breakthrough philosophy. Naomi Klein describes disaster capitalism. Piketty labours to explain the new inequality. Vandana Shiva sermonises on the seed. But in truth we have retreated from the commons, the demos, the zocalo. We have accepted the globalisation of capital. We have allowed the unjust wars to continue. We have witnessed the flow of refugees around the world. We have allowed the rule of law to wane. We no longer champion aid and development in poorer countries. We have not fought for the public space, for the collective, for the Common Wealth. We have voted for Opportunity over Outcome.

Yet we, the children born in the 1960s, are no different from previous generations. No different in our bones to our boomer parents born in the post war explosion, when fridges and station wagons sprouted in the suburbs as the atom bomb framed a cold war between the USSR and USA. We know the same things, we understand injustice, we are ready to be heroic. We are ready to apply the lessons, to live the example of Mandela or JFK or maybe just Jackie Onassis. Some of us have a hipster sense that style itself will redeem our species. We may live unfairly and unequally but hey, in a pillbox hat with a cigarette holder and an Austin Healey sports car anything can be excused. Yes!

We are adrift from each other, unable to come together properly to change the outer world to better match our inner worlds. Perhaps a collective mid-life crisis can change that? The best I can come up with is that we need to Rebuild Our Common Wealth. Can we give that a go?

A Brain Dump of Our Problems

Child poverty. Home ownership. Indigenous imprisonment rates. Women killed at home. Dry rivers. Criminalising dissent. A dying reef. Declining press freedom. Union bashing. House prices. Wage stagnation. Water theft. Foreign policy. Rents. No treaty. Poor infrastructure. Youth unemployment. Renewable energy. Abuse of refugees. Standard of debate. Imperialism. Contempt for institutions. Everything is politicised. Mental health. All is soundbite. The future has been abolished. One scandal after another. Underpaid workers. Everything is personalised. Political violence. Bad mines. Public housing. Buying submarines. Politicians tobogganing down the grass over Parliament House while We the People cannot. Work in progress.

Please add to this list. Then return to *Part Six: Seriously. Fixing Australia.* to work on your solutions to all them. Methodically. Patiently. Effectively. Come on. Let's do this!

PART TEN:
Exercises to Make Australia Slightly Better Than Average Again™

1. Make a list of policies you would introduce if you ran the Government of Australia. Limit yourself to ten because we need to be ruthlessly realistic, ok?

2. Walk into the street and make a little list of things you see in public space, from the roads and gutters, to the hospitals and cars. Next to each item, write down the estimated cost and who funds each thing you are looking at. If you have time, make a note of the things that need work and who might fix them and who will pay for it.

3. Sit down in front of a screen and watch a news program. Make a list of the numbers provided from the stock exchange indexes to the temperatures, from the road toll to the sports scores. Make a list of things you would actually like reports and numbers on.

4. Learn the Gumatj verses of the song *Treaty* by Yothu Yindi. Then teach the song to someone you know. Or a total stranger.

5. Sit down with a calculator and work out your wage or salary ten years ago, what you paid in tax then and what you could buy with your money, and then do the same thing with what you earn now. Try to work out the impact of tax cuts on your life.

6. Do the Exercise entitled Dilating the Cervix of Our Glorious Nation in Part Seven.

7. Pub quiz. OK. Ready. Your time starts now . . .

   a) Is Australia an economy or a society?
   b) Do human beings mainly compete or co-operate?
   c) Should we govern or let the market sort everything out?

8. Find Peter Dutton. Invite him to hug you. You might want to ring his office first and make an appointment. Peter might need to prepare. But when you get together, open your arms good and wide, welcoming the Minister for Home Affairs into your warm embrace. Ask Peter the one simple question: 'where does it hurt?'. This is radical compassion in action. Australia will never be the same again.

9. Take the day off. If you have kids, ring in sick for them, make a pizza together (including the dough) and some home-made lemonade. Then sit down and watch parliament together. I would recommend Question Time or Senate Estimates. Prepare your children with a brief explanation that these are the people who run our country and are planning for your future. Photograph their reactions. Pin the images to the fridge.

10. Drinking game. At the pub, wine bar or football club function, take turns to explain The Australian Economy to each other. All players have a maximum of 3 minutes each. No powerpoint, no whiteboard, no googling. Penalty shots for waffling. Good luck!

Acknowledgments . . .

Huge thanks to . . . Heather Stevenson, Mark Foster, John Davies, David Musgrave and Ed Wright for bringing this book to the page. To Anne Coombs, Colleen Ryan and Mandy Nolan for their support and encouragement. To Kathryn, Thibault and Nina for looking after me. To Aubrey, always. And to everyone at Eureka FC who started this Indian summer.

Author's Note . . .

Writing this book has created a political party. It is called *Together*. Like minded friends and total strangers are joining as you read this. We will try to implement the ideas of this book in the real world of #auspol. We aim to run candidates in the 2019 federal election. Find us at: thetogetherparty.org.au or on Facebook @Together. The Party. or @Senator Swiv. Or email me at mark@swivel.net.au. I would love to hear from you.

Mark Swivel, 1 November 2018

Printed in Australia
AUHW010955280819
316567AU00001B/2